D0043571

THE JOY of PRAYER

A 40-Day Devotional to Invigorate Your Prayer Life

WITH A COMPANION GUIDE FOR GROUP STUDY

Dr. Alvin VanderGriend

PRAYERSHOP PUBLISHING

Terre Haute, Indiana
www.prayershop.org

PrayerShop Publishing is the publishing arm of Harvest Prayer Ministries and the Church Prayer Leaders Network. Harvest Prayer Ministries exists to make every church a house of prayer. Its online prayer store—www.prayershop.org—offers more than 400 prayer resources for purchase.

Cover design: Pamela Poll
Text design: Pamela Poll
Editor: Don Mcrory, Marjo Jordan

© 2007, 1st printing, Alvin J. VanderGriend

All rights reserved. Except for brief excerpts for review or educational purposes, no part of this book may be reproduced in any manner whatsoever without written permission from the publisher.

Unless otherwise indicated, Scripture quotations in this publication are from the HOLY BIBLE, NEW INTERNATIONAL VERSION © 1973, 1978, 1984, International Bible Society. Used by permission of Zondervan Publishing House. All rights reserved.

Published in cooperation with:
Alvin J. VanderGriend
606 Woodcreek Drive
Lynden, WA 98264

1 2 3 4 5 6 7 8 9 10 | 12 11 10 09 08 07

Five Ways to Use
The Joy of Prayer

1. Personal Devotions

Many people use *The Joy of Prayer* for personal devotions as a way to invigorate their prayer lives. Those who gain the most work through the segments "Something to Think About," "Something to Pray About," and "Something to Act On."

2. Family Devotions

Whole families gain prayer strength and depth by using *The Joy of Prayer* for regular family devotions—usually at mealtimes. Family members take turns reading aloud. They discuss the "Think" questions, use the "Pray" prompts to enrich their family prayer times, and agree to try one or more of the "Something to Act On" suggestions each week.

3. Prayer Cells

Prayer cells use *The Joy of Prayer* to stimulate their prayer times together. Cell members decide in advance which devotional readings to use each week. They then act on what they have learned and put it into practice when they meet.

4. Small Groups and Education Classes

Small groups and education classes use the companion study guide along with the 40 devotional readings in *The Joy of Prayer*. Each study session includes a DVD introduction, group interaction questions, Bible study, and a closing prayer time. The following week, small group members put their learning into practice by doing the "Personal Prayer This Week" and reading the five devotionals that correspond with the study guide theme.

5. Whole Church

Most churches initiate a 40-day prayer emphasis using the 40-day devotional book, *Love to Pray* (also written by Alvin VanderGriend). The basic content of *Love to Pray* lends itself well to *40 Days of Prayer*. However, *The Joy of*

Prayer—though dealing with more advanced prayer topics--will also work for a whole church, 40-day prayer emphasis.

In the whole church emphasis, individual members or families use the forty devotionals on their own. The pastor preaches on the weekly prayer themes. Small groups, home cells, or church education classes use the companion study guide for their sessions. Specially planned prayer activities give all the members of the church prayer-learning experiences. A *40 Days of Prayer Resource Kit*, which includes *Strategy Guidelines* is available from PrayerShop Publishing (www.prayershop. org or 800-217-5200).

Preface

The idea for this book was born out of my personal experience in discovering the joy of prayer. Having discovered this joy, I then searched the Bible for affirmation. Not surprisingly, I found Bible writers regularly linking joy with prayer and prayer with joy.

One of the first things I noticed in this study was how all of the elements of prayer are connected with joy. Worshipers experience joy in *praise* as they "Shout for joy to the LORD . . . worship the LORD with gladness," and "come before him with joyful songs" (Psalm 100:1-2). Believers, blessed with the spiritual riches of God's grace, "joyfully *give thanks* to the Father" (Colossians 1:11-12). David senses his *confession* turning to joy as he pleads with God to "restore to me the joy of your salvation" (Psalm 51:12). And Jesus promises that *asking* will lead to "complete joy" for those who *ask* in his name and receive what they ask (John 16:23-24). Even *fasting*—a type of prayer usually associated with weeping and mourning—can be turned into a "joyful and glad occasion" (Zechariah 8:19).

I further discovered how joy was at the very heart of the experience of believers who came to God's "house of prayer"—the temple in Jerusalem. Isaiah tells us that God, who brought foreigners to his holy mountain to worship him, gave them "joy in his house of prayer" (Isaiah 56:7). Their joy was the joy of coming near to God and experiencing his presence. Their experience was similar to that of David's who wrote: "You will fill me with joy in your presence, with eternal pleasures at your right hand" (Psalm 16:11).

Other prayer themes developed in this book should also increase joy in your prayer life. Imagine the joy of "Hearing God in Prayer"! Imagine gaining victory over the enemy in "Prayer and Spiritual Warfare"! Winning gives us reason to celebrate—especially winning over the devil and his demonic forces. Jesus, the Supreme Joy-Giver, promises to be present when two or three come together in prayer as part of the "The Praying Church." How much joy is *that*! God provides many ways to give us joy. You'll notice how often these ways are related to prayer.

THE JOY OF PRAYER WITH STUDY GUIDE

The bottom line is simply this: The joy of prayer is the joy of meeting God, of conversing with God, and of living in an ongoing, love relationship with him. It's impossible to come into God's presence, as we do in prayer, and not experience joy. It is my hope you will find in the pages of this devotional book, thoughts on prayer and experiences in prayer that will greatly increase your joy of prayer.

Joyfully and prayerfully,

Alvin Vander Griend

Contents

WEEK ONE

THE JOY OF PRAYER

The Joy of Prayer

The foreigners who bind themselves to the Lord to serve him, to love the name of the Lord, and to worship him, all who keep the Sabbath without desecrating it and who hold fast to my covenant—these I will bring to my holy mountain and give them joy in my house of prayer.
ISAIAH 56:6-7

True joy is joy in God. No joy on earth can compare with the joy we have in God. This joy is the joy of knowing God and living in a love relationship with him. David had a taste of it when he said to God: "You will fill me with joy in your presence, with eternal pleasures at your right hand" (Ps. 16:11).

Joy is also a gift that Christ promises us. He too connected joy to a love relationship. After telling his disciples how to remain in his love he said, "I have told you this so that my joy may be in you and that your joy may be complete" (John 15:11).

Prayer is a pathway to joy because it involves us in a love relationship with God. In my previous book, *Love to Pray*, I defined prayer as "the conversational part of the most important love relationship in our life—our love relationship with the Father, the Son and the Holy Spirit" (p. 8). It's impossible to talk with or listen to God and not, in the end, experience joy.

It shouldn't surprise us, then, that prayer and joy meet head on in a place—that place where Old Testament believers met God—in the temple at Jerusalem. God said of those who came to meet him there, "I will . . . give them joy in my house of prayer."

The joy people experienced in God's "house of prayer" was the joy of prayer. The temple was the place where God chose to dwell. For more than a thousand years the temple in Jerusalem stood as the place where God's people came into his presence and communicated with him. Though not visible, God was really there. Those who came to the temple came to meet God. And because they met him they experienced joy.

Everything about the temple spoke of prayer. The altar of incense in the holy place was an altar of prayer. The smoke of the incense that rose upward from it symbolized ascending prayers. The required offerings—the burnt offering, meal offering, peace offering, sin offering, and guilt offering—were really acted-out prayers, each one touching a different aspect of the believer's relationship with God.

Today we can have the same joyful experience in prayer that people who went to that earthly "house of prayer" had, and we don't have to go to a place to meet him. God the Father, through the atoning death of his Son Jesus, has provided a new and living way for us to come freely into his presence. We can come to him in prayer anytime, anywhere, about anything, and in so doing we always will know the joy of prayer.

Sometimes, however, our prayers feel anything but joyful. How can we be joyful when our prayers of confession are filled with sorrow over sin, or when our hearts are breaking over a tragic loss? How can we experience joy when our prayers come out of the depths of despair or when God says "no" to what we deeply desire?

The truth is that even prayers that arise out of heartbreak and despair will end with joy if we let God meet us and minister to us in the midst of our distresses. It is precisely because prayer brings us to God that it can bring us from sorrow to joy. Jesus himself traveled such a path as he journeyed from the depths of sorrow in Gethsemane, through the agony of death on cross, and then on to Easter joy and a glorious ascension to God's right hand. Our paths will lead there too.

Something to **Think** About
◆ Why do you think that meeting God in prayer gives us joy?
◆ When has prayer been a joyful experience for you? Has it ever seemed like a drag? What made the difference?
◆ Have you ever started a time of prayer feeling really bad and then ended up feeling really joyful? How did that happen?

Something to **Pray** About
◆ *Praise* God as the joy-giver.
◆ *Thank* God for prayer and the freedom of access it gives you into his presence where there is fullness of joy.
◆ *Confess* if you find yourself seeking joy in the wrong ways or the wrong places.
◆ *Ask* God for a deeper richer prayer life and the joy that comes with it.

Something to **Act** On
In the next couple of weeks ask God to make you aware that you are really meeting *him* every time you pray. Ask him to give you the same joy as he gave to those who came to his "house of prayer."

The Joy of Praise

Shout for joy to the Lord, all the earth. Worship the Lord with gladness;
come before him with joyful songs. Know that the Lord is God.
PSALM 100:1-3

Joy is at the very heart of God's plan for human beings. He knows that we are aching for joy. He wants us to have the joy of knowing him and being in his presence. Praise is one way that God gives us his joy. Praise gives rise to joy because praise makes God real to us!

Praise is a heartfelt response to *who God is*. Thanksgiving is a response to *what God gives*. Be sure that you don't confuse the two. When we give thanks our thoughts still revolve around ourselves and what we may get from God. When we praise him our thoughts focus entirely on God.

The joy of praise is really joy *in* God. It is responding to *who he is*. The Westminster Shorter Catechism reminds us that our chief purpose on earth is "to glorify God and enjoy him forever." Glorifying God and enjoying him are not two separate things. They are inseparably linked. To glorify God *is* to enjoy him. To enjoy him *is* to glorify him. Both lead us into an experience with God.

God is the most enjoyable person in the world. He is the source of all true joy. He reveals his beauty and his glory to us so that we can lovingly enjoy him. As we get in touch with him, his joy flows into our lives.

The Scriptures are packed with joyful praise to God. Nehemiah speaks of those who "delight in revering [God's] name" (1:11).The prophet Isaiah professes, "I delight greatly in the Lord; my soul rejoices in my God" (61:10). Psalm 100 invites us to "shout for joy to the Lord, all the earth. Worship the Lord with gladness; come before him with joyful songs. Know that the Lord is God" (Ps. 100:1-3). Those who praise God always seem to find a spring of joy bubbling up within their hearts.

Praise opens the door for God's joy to flood into our lives. Several years ago I was led to begin spending extended time on Sunday mornings just praising God and being in his presence. It started with fifteen minutes; then it was half an hour; then forty-five minutes; and finally an hour. I now find this hour to be the most delightful and refreshing hour of the week. Though getting up early isn't easy for me, when Sunday morning rolls around I find myself hopping out of bed with the thought: "This is my morning to spend an hour just enjoying God."

Praising God not only gives *us* joy; it gives *God* joy too. As we enjoy him he enjoys us and takes pleasure in the fact that we find joy in him. We are God's precious children; and we have the ability to gladden our Father's heart. The prophet Zephaniah discloses just how good we can make God feel: "He will take great delight in you . . . he will rejoice over you with singing" (Zeph. 3:17). Imagine that! Maybe there are times—when we are singing a hymn like "Rejoice in the Lord Always"—that God in heaven is singing too, except that he is putting your name into his song.

Would you like to be a radiant, joyful Christian? Then you must learn to enjoy God. Take time to focus your attention on him—his beauty, his glory, his majesty, his splendor, his holiness. Reflect back to him what you see. Make sure he knows how much you appreciate him for *who he is*. Not to praise God is to act as if he doesn't exist. To act as if God doesn't exist is to be a practical atheist; and atheists definitely do not enjoy God.

Something to **Think** About

- ◆ Do you experience God's joy as a trickle, a stream, a river, or a flood? What would it take for you to increase the measure of joy you experience in your relationship with God?
- ◆ What is there about God that you find most enjoyable? Take time to tell him about that right now.

Something to **Pray** About

- ◆ *Praise* God as the joy-giver. Tell him how much you appreciate and enjoy him.
- ◆ *Thank* the Father for his joy-plan. *Thank* the Son for his gift of joy (John 16:24). *Thank* the Holy Spirit for the fruit of joy (Gal. 5:22).
- ◆ *Confess* if you have failed to rejoice in the Lord and to take delight in him.
- ◆ *Ask* God to give you the time and the desire to praise, adore, and enjoy him.

Something to **Act** On

Dedicate an extended time to praise this week. Meditate on passages like 1 Chronicles 29:10-13; Psalm 9:1-2, 7-9; Psalm 145:1-7; Romans 11:33-36; and Revelation 4:11. Write out your own prayers of praise.

Adopt the basic rule: "No supplication for the first five minutes" for your personal or small group prayer times.

The Joy of Thanksgiving

We pray . . . that you may live a life worthy of the Lord and may please
him in every way: . . . joyfully giving thanks to the Father.
COL. 1:10-12

It is a joy to give thanks to God. In Paul's way of thinking, joy and thanksgiving come together. His prayer for the Colossian Christians is that they be
able to "joyfully give thanks to the Father." In another letter he urges all believers to "be joyful always; pray continually; give thanks in all circumstances"
(1 Thess. 5:16-18). The joy of thanksgiving is possible anytime and anywhere.
It comes from an awareness of the Father's good gifts and his gracious generosity toward us all.

Thanksgiving is a heartfelt response to *what God gives*. When we praise
him we respond to *who God is;* we see his face. When we give thanks, we see
God's open hand and respond with joyful hearts to his generosity.

Thanksgiving naturally gives rise to joy. It causes us to be conscious of God
and what he has done. God is so good and has done so much for us that the
thought of his good gifts produces joy.

Joy, on the other hand, can give rise to thanksgiving. David celebrates the
joy of a divine healing with a commitment to continuous thanksgiving: "You
turned my wailing into dancing; you removed my sackcloth and clothed me
with joy, that my heart may sing to you and not be silent. O Lord my God, I
will give you thanks forever" (Ps. 30:11-12).

The Scriptures suggest a number of practical ways to increase thanksgiving. First, they teach us to give thanks for the *people* through whom God has
blessed our lives. Paul's example is very compelling. Eight times in his letters
he gives thanks for those to whom he is writing. He says to the Thessalonians,
"We always thank God for all of you, mentioning you in our prayers" (1
Thess. 1:2). Think of the people whom God has used to touch your life for
good—parents, grandparents, children, relatives, friends, teachers, neighbors,
or coworkers—and give thanks for them.

Second, be aware of and give thanks for *spiritual blessings*. We tend to be so
consumed by things that we almost forget the spiritual blessings that literally
fill our lives—new birth, faith, grace, mercy, love, joy, peace, hope, wisdom,

strength, guidance, knowledge, prayer, worship, and the like. All of these things come from God who has given us "everything we need for life and godliness" (2 Peter 1:3). If we regularly thank God for spiritual blessings we will never lack a reason for giving thanks.

Third, give thanks for blessings of *the past*. One reason God has given us memory is so that we can recall past blessings. Psalm 105, for example, includes more than 40 verses recalling how God blessed his people from the time they left Egypt until they entered the Promised Land. Verses 1 and 3 set the stage with these words: "Give thanks to the Lord . . . let the hearts of those who seek the Lord rejoice." I have found that giving thanks for past blessings always brings great joy to my heart.

Fourth, make thankful prayer a *lifestyle*. "Always [give] thanks to God the Father for everything," writes Paul in Ephesians 5:20. God's good gifts come as a constant flow—life, breath, health, friends, family, food, protection, Christ, the Holy Spirit, salvation, and a thousand things more. If we recognize these as gifts of God's love it will be natural for us to give thanks for everything and to experience the joy of thanksgiving.

Not to be thankful is like saying to God, "I don't need you. You're no help. I am doing fine without you and your gifts." Such arrogance has no place in the life of the praying Christian.

Something to **Think** About

◆ How often do you experience the joy of thanksgiving? What one thing can you do to increase it?

◆ Which one of the four practical suggestions comes easiest for you? Which one is the hardest? Why?

Something to **Pray** About

◆ *Praise* God as the giver of "every good and perfect gift" (James 1:17).

◆ *Thank* God for all the spiritual blessings you can think of. *Thank* him for the people he has used to bless your life.

◆ If you have been too little aware of God's gifts and have tended to take him for granted, *confess* that as sin.

◆ *Ask* God for a grateful heart and a fresh awareness of his goodness to you and yours.

Something to **Act** On

Make a list of the spiritual blessings (start with those mentioned in the devotional) and thank God for each one. Tell God what that gift has meant to you.

The Joy of Confession

O God . . . blot out my transgressions. Wash away all my iniquity and
cleanse me from my sin. . . . Let me hear joy and gladness. . . . Restore to
me the joy of your salvation and grant me a willing spirit, to sustain me.
PSALM 51:1-2, 8, 12

To talk about the *joy* of *confession* seems like an oxymoron—a combination of contradictory ideas. In a way it is. Confession of sin is never joyful. It is always painful. In fact the Bible challenges sinners: "Change your laughter to mourning and your joy to gloom" (James 4:9).

But in another way it isn't. There is a direct link between confession and joy. Twice in Psalm 51 David links joy to the removal of sin. In verse 8 he writes, "Let me hear joy and gladness." And in verse 12 we read these words: "Restore to me the joy of my salvation." Confession moves us from pain to joy, from gloom to gladness.

I used to think of confession as the most unpleasant part of prayer. It was like the foul-tasting cod-liver oil my mother gave me when I was sick. But as I came to understand confession better I began to think of it more like a piece of candy that was sour on the outside but sweet on the inside. You start with the sour taste, but soon get to the sweetness.

Nothing squelches joy more than sin. Sin leads to the uncomfortable and joyless feelings of guilt, shame, anxiety, and fear. It disrupts our relationship with God. Isaiah charges: "Your iniquities have separated you from your God; your sins have hidden his face from you, so that he will not hear" (59:2).

Sin disrupts our relationship with God, but confession restores it. That's why confession can lead to joy. It leads us through a change of mind called repentance, and through a change of life called conversion. As did the prophet Isaiah, we will hear God say, "Your guilt is taken away and your sin atoned for" (Is. 6:7). Those words open a door to life at its best, life full of health and joy.

To confess means to see our sins as God sees them, to hate them as God hates them, and to oppose them as God in his wrath opposes them. Taking such an attitude toward our sin does not lead to shame, as one might assume, but to cleansing, release, and joy.

To be sure, confession is not popular in our culture today. We tend to shrink from sincere confession of sin. We prefer to call a sin a mistake, a blunder, or a foul-up. We learn to compare ourselves with "gross" sinners and in so doing we come off looking pretty good. All of this is just a cover-up.

Covering up sin is a sign of weakness; confessing sin is a sign of strength. Solomon had it right when he wrote: "He who conceals his sins does not prosper, but whoever confesses and renounces them finds mercy" (Prov. 28:13). Covering up sin is like denying having cancer though tests confirm it. Confessing sin is like admitting having cancer and then receiving treatment. Confession works healing that leads to wholeness.

God designed prayer as a way for us to have intimate, joyous fellowship with him. Sin hampers that intimacy. Confession restores it. For David, confession restored joy because it restored his relationship with God.

God always welcomes confession because he wants a close relationship with us. He wants to repair the effects of sin; wants to remove the cancer that hinders our relationship with him. Confession of sin allows our loving Father to work the miracle of his grace and to restore our joy and peace. It gives *him* joy to restore *our* joy.

Something to **Think** About
◆ Have you tended to think of confession as *bitter* or *sweet*?
◆ Think of a time in your life when sin hampered joy. Did joy get restored? How did that happen?
◆ How should a parent respond to a child's sincere confession of wrongdoing? What kind of changes would come out of that?

Something to **Pray** About
◆ *Praise* God for his mercy—the compassion he has in the face of human need.
◆ *Ask* the Holy Spirit to search your heart for any sins that may be the cause of obstructed joy.
◆ *Confess* any sin that has robbed you of joy in your relationship with God. Accept God's forgiving grace.
◆ *Thank* Jesus for his atoning death on the cross by which your sins are forgiven and your heart cleansed.

Something to **Act** On
Take some relaxed time to read and meditate on Psalm 51. Let the Spirit teach you important things about confession and restoration from its verses.

The Joy of Asking

I tell you the truth, my Father will give you whatever you ask in my name. Until now you have not asked for anything in my name. Ask and you will receive, and your joy will be complete.
JOHN 16:23-24

Jesus thought asking should be joyful. "Ask," he said, "and you will receive, and your joy will be complete." Wow!

Asking God for things, however, isn't always enjoyable. Praying through lists of prayer requests can be boring. When others lead in prayer and ask for things that we are not interested in our minds wander. And what about the times we ask and ask and ask and do not receive. That isn't very enjoyable.

How are we supposed to understand Jesus' promise that asking leads to joy? The explanation is in the phrase "in my name." Jesus didn't say that asking alone would give us joy. What he said was that asking "in his name" would give us joy.

Asking in Jesus' name is much more than adding the words "in Jesus' name" to the end of our prayers. It means that we come to the Father with new hearts and Spirit-cleansed lives; that we come as spokespersons for Christ; and that we come asking for the very things that Christ desires—those things that will bring glory to the Father and build his kingdom. When we come that way we *will* receive what we ask for and *will* have complete joy.

That wasn't how the disciples asked. They asked in an Old Testament way, which meant that they based their prayers on the promises God had made to Abraham, Isaac, and Jacob. Now Jesus is offering them a better way to pray—"in his name."

We experience "complete joy" when asking in this way for several reasons. First, asking is communication with our heavenly Father who is "the love of our life." To ask him is to step into the atmosphere of his love. It is to be reminded that he loves us "with an everlasting love" (Jer. 31:3) and that he is both willing and able to give us what we ask.

We also experience joy in asking because we receive what we ask for. When we ask in accord with God's will we can have everything God has promised—everything, that is, "we need for life and godliness" (2 Peter 1:3). We can have the graces that we need for spiritual growth: faith, hope, love, wisdom, guidance, insight, joy, and peace. We can have the power to be effective in ministry. We can have Christ, the hope of glory (Col. 1:27). Asking and receiving is very exciting when we draw on God's sufficiency to supply our needs.

We will also find joy in asking when we ask for others. When we pray for others we partner with God in providing his blessing. At seminars I often give attendees five minutes to pray silently for persons they know who are not yet followers of Christ. When invited to share what they experienced when praying this way attendees often say, "I had a feeling of joy." When I ask why the usual response is something like: "I know God will be doing things in their lives because I prayed." What they experience at that moment is the joy of asking.

Maybe asking has not always been joyful for you. Not all asking is joyful. But asking "in Jesus' name" and getting what we ask for from our loving heavenly Father is joyful. "Taste and see that the Lord is good," wrote David in Psalm 34:8. So is your mouth watering?

Something to **Think** About

◆ When have you recently experienced joy in asking? Was it the joy of sensing the Father's love, the joy of receiving what you asked for, or the joy of blessing another person?

◆ What could you do to make sure that you are always *really* praying in Jesus' name?

Something to **Pray** About

◆ *Praise* the Father for his willingness to give you whatever you ask in the name of his Son.

◆ *Thank* God for this wonderful New Testament way of praying.

◆ *Ask* the Holy Spirit to teach you what and how to pray in accord with God's will.

◆ *Commit* yourself to edit out of your prayers anything that is selfishly motivated and not in accord with God's will.

Something to **Act** On

Use most of your prayer time asking for things that you know will glorify the Father, build his kingdom, and strengthen your spiritual life.

WEEK TWO

PRAYING WITH THE TRINITY

Praying *to* the Father

This, then, is how you should pray: "Our Father in heaven. . . ."
MATTHEW 6:9

The first lesson Jesus taught us about prayer was how to address God. Though we think of God as "God," that is not really his name. "God" is a title that means "strong one." Had Jesus taught us to start our prayers saying "Our God in heaven" he would have distorted our understanding of God.

But Jesus didn't teach us to pray "Our God in heaven." He taught us to pray "Our Father in heaven." "Father" is not his name either. It describes his role. It is a form of address that defines a relationship—the Father-child relationship into which Jesus brings us. If God is our Father then we are his dear children and prayer is a personal conversation with our Father. This makes all the difference in the world as we go into God's presence in prayer.

What we believe about God has a telling effect on our prayers. If we think of God as a celestial Santa Claus, our prayers will consist of asking. If we think of God as a doting grandparent, our prayers will not contain much confession. If we think of God as a stern judge, then we will want to stay far away from him and his courtroom. But, if he is truly "Our Father," lavishing his love on us and treating us as his children (1 John 3:1), then prayer will always be a love relationship filled with tender affection and trust. That's what Jesus intended.

As far as we know, Jesus was the first person ever to call God "Father." He often spoke of God as *his* Father. He began every one of his earthly prayers, except the prayer of agony from the cross, by addressing him as Father. He understood that his Father was very fond of him and loved him with an everlasting love. What's more, Jesus took pains to make it clear to us that we too can be children of God and know him personally as *our* Father. In fact, it was Jesus who gave us "the right to become children of God" (John 1:12).

The loving Father-child relationship that is so highly important to us, is also important to the Father. As a Father he wants to be close to us, longs to interact with us and is delighted when we talk to him. He loves us and is devoted to us. He finds joy in having an ongoing and growing love relationship with us.

It's important for us to remember that the Father-child relationship into which we step when we pray "Our Father" is not a relationship of equals. He is the Father, we are the children. He is "in heaven" and we are on earth. He is uncontained by and greater than the universe. We are finite and limited.

The fact that the Father is infinitely superior to us his children is a huge advantage for us. He who is our almighty, all-wise and loving Father is "for us." He unleashes his supernatural power on our behalf to save us from sin, to protect us from evil, to bless us, and to provide an eternal heavenly home for us.

It's okay and even valuable for us, when we pray, to use the other titles and names of God. But, no matter how we address God, we should never forget that he is our gracious heavenly Father and that we are his beloved sons and daughters.

As the truest and best of fathers our Abba is always delighted when we come to him. We can rightly say that prayer is the conversational part of the most important Father-child love relationship in our lives.

Something to **Think** About

◆ When you pray what difference does it make for you to know that God is your Father?

◆ What do you suppose your heavenly Father is thinking and feeling when you come to him in prayer with childlike love?

Something to **Pray** About

◆ *Praise* your Father in heaven for his unconditional love.

◆ *Thank* your Abba for loving you, caring for you, providing for you, and always seeking your best.

◆ If you have grieved your Father by giving him too little of your heart, your life, or your love, *confess* that and ask him to forgive you.

◆ *Ask* the Holy Spirit to help you know how great the Father's love is that he has lavished upon you.

Something to **Act** On

Develop a brief seven- to eight-word prayer that reminds you of your heavenly Father's love for you. Pray that prayer often throughout the day. Some examples: "Father, I belong to you." "Father, I am yours, you are mine." "Abba, you're the love of my life."

Praying *Through* the Son

Therefore [Jesus] is able to save completely those who come to God through him, because he always lives to intercede for them.
HEBREWS 7:25

God the Father has always wanted a close relationship with his children. When the children of Israel traveled from Egypt to the Promised Land he traveled with them in a cloud and had them pitch a tent for him. When they settled in Canaan he dwelt with them, first in the tabernacle at Shiloh, and then in the temple at Jerusalem.

But because of sin he could not allow them to get close to him. Gentile seekers who came to Jerusalem had to stay way away from him in the temple's outer courtyard. Ceremonially pure Jews could come somewhat closer in the inner courtyard. Ordained priests were allowed still closer as they ministered in the holy place of the temple. But a thick curtain cordoned off God's dwelling place in the holy of holies even for the priests. Only the high priest could go into the presence of God in the holy of holies, and that only once a year after complicated rites of purification. So risky was this approach to God that a scarlet cord was attached to the high priest's leg so his body could be removed if something went wrong.

The problem was, and still is, that God, in his supreme holiness, cannot allow a sinful person into his presence. Sinners simply cannot be in God's presence and live.

So what did God do in order to have a close love relationship with his sinful children? He made a way for sin to be removed from us. He sent Jesus to take our sins upon himself and to atone for them by dying in our place on the cross. In this way our sinful hearts are cleansed by the Holy Spirit who dwells within us. With sin gone God no longer has to hold us at a distance. The barriers that once kept people away are removed. The "cordoning" curtain is torn in two. The way into God's presence is open. His children can now come close to him without fear. And they have the freedom to come not just once a year, or even once in a while, but any time of any day.

This is the "opening" that was needed to make it possible for us to come to God in prayer and to enjoy life's most important love relationship, our love relationship with the Father made possible through the Son.

The writer to the Hebrews describes it this way: "We have confidence to enter the Most Holy Place . . . by a new and living way opened for us through the curtain" (Heb. 10:19-20). Jesus is the way into the Father's presence; the way to the Father's heart. In other words, in prayer we come *to* the Father *through* the Son.

The access we have to the Father through the Son is life's highest privilege, life's greatest glory. And, praise the Lord, it is a privilege that will never be taken away from any true believer. Jesus is in God's throne room constantly interceding on our behalf. He is "able to save completely those who come to God through him." Every time you or I pray, Jesus is there at the Father's right hand waiting to hear from us, waiting to take our prayers to the Father. He keeps the door open. Nothing on earth or in heaven can ever bar the way to the Father's throne as long as Jesus is there holding the door open.

Jesus "always lives to intercede for us." He is engaged in that all the time. He is there right now speaking up for you, carrying your prayers to the Father. What a wonderful Savior!

Something to **Think** About

♦ Try to think of yourself in the throne room of heaven. What difference does that make when you pray?

♦ If you could see the face of Jesus as he takes your prayers to the Father, what do you think would be "written" on it?

Something to **Pray** About

♦ *Praise* Jesus Christ, the Son of God, who is alive right now and is interceding for you.

♦ *Thank* Jesus for being your friend and representative at the right hand of the Father.

♦ *Confess* any sin that might keep God from listening to you (Ps. 66:18).

♦ *Ask* the Father to give you an increased awareness to be in his presence in the Throne Room.

Something to **Act** On

Read Hebrews 7:23-8:2, 9:11-15, and 10:19-25 in a contemporary version and meditate on these verses to get a more complete picture of the high priestly ministry of Christ and the privilege you have to draw near to God through him.

Praying by the Spirit

And pray in the Spirit on all occasions.
EPH. 6:18
Build yourselves up . . . and pray in the Holy Spirit.
JUDE 20

We pray *to* the Father. We pray *through* the Son. We pray *by* the Holy Spirit. All three persons of the Trinity are involved with us in prayer. Each has a specific role. Each works in harmony with the other two and, at the same time, with us as we pray.

The New Testament twice urges us to "pray in the Spirit." That sounds like a command but it's really an offer of grace. The phrase "pray in the Spirit" literally means "pray as enabled by the Spirit." In other words, we are not commanded to pray in some spiritual way; we are offered help by the Spirit to pray as God intended.

It's good that we have the Spirit to help us too. Otherwise we wouldn't be able to pray very well at all. Paul acknowledges as much when he says in Romans 8:26, "We do not know how to pray as we should" (NASB). However, he says, "the Spirit helps us in our weakness." God's answer to our inability to pray as we should is to give us the Holy Spirit as our "prayer helper."

A lot of praying that goes on in the Christian community today seems flawed. I hear a lot of asking, but little praising. There seems to be a great deal more talking to God, than listening. Our prayers are so filled with what's on our minds, that we're hardly aware of what's on God's mind.

But it doesn't have to be that way. When the Spirit takes over in our prayer lives, things change. He adds depth and power and faith to our prayers. He helps us listen. He reveals the heart of God. He supplies everything we need to know to pray as we should.

The Holy Spirit is our indwelling prayer assistant. He longs for our prayer lives to be powerful and effective. He is able to help us with all kinds of prayer. He moves us to *praise* by making us aware of God's wonderful ways. He brings us to our knees in *confession* by searching our hearts and convicting us of sin. He induces prayers of *thanksgiving* by helping us see and know the good gifts that the Father gives. He prompts prayers of *intercession* by opening our eyes

26

to the needs of a hurting world. He rouses us to *petition* for spiritual blessings by holding before us the Father's promise of "good gifts" for those who ask.

The Holy Spirit also links us to Christ—the only perfect pray-er this world has ever known. He stands ready and willing to help us pray as Christ prayed and to connect us to the ongoing intercessory ministry of Christ.

With the Spirit's help our prayer lives can be transformed from duty to delight, from a formula to fondness for the Father, from a method to a meeting with God. With the Spirit's energy surging within us we can pray more fervently, more earnestly, more boldly, and more persistently. By means of the Spirit's enabling power we *can* pray "on all occasions with all kinds of prayers and requests" (Eph. 6:18).

What a helper the Holy Spirit is! He is almighty and all-wise. He knows everything there is to know about prayer and is ready, willing, and able to teach us everything he knows. There is no reason for us to be powerless and ineffective in prayer. The Father will give the Holy Spirit to all who ask and the Spirit will help all who want to deepen their prayer lives. You *can be* the kind of pray-er God wants you to be. It's a promise—a promise from God.

Something to **Think** About

◆ Is prayer a duty or a delight for you? A formula or a fondness for the Father? A method or a meeting with God?

◆ What kind of help with prayer do you most need from the Holy Spirit? How will you go about getting it?

Something to **Pray** About

◆ *Praise* the Holy Spirit as a wonderful, God-given, indwelling prayer helper.

◆ *Thank* the Spirit for all the help he has given you with prayer.

◆ *Confess* anything that you have done to grieve the Spirit, especially as he tried to help you grow stronger in prayer.

◆ *Ask* the Holy Spirit to help you pray as you should. Be specific about the kind of help you need.

Something to **Act** On

Start each of your formal prayer times in the next few days by asking the Holy Spirit to help you pray as you should. Pause to listen. Then begin to pray following his lead rather than a familiar pattern.

Praying *for* the Spirit

If you then, though you are evil, know how to give good gifts to your
children, how much more will your Father in heaven give the Holy
Spirit to those who ask him!
                                    LUKE 11:13

It's one thing to pray *by* the Holy Spirit. It's another thing to pray *for* the
Holy Spirit. As we learned in the previous devotional, the Holy Spirit is the
Father's gift to help us pray. Now we take another step and see that the Spirit is
also the Father's primary gift to assist us in our spiritual lives.

Before Jesus ascended to heaven he promised that he would send the Holy
Spirit (Luke 24:49). He fulfilled that promise when he and the Father poured
out the Spirit on the church on the day of Pentecost. However, Jesus also
taught us to *ask for* the Holy Spirit. Comparing the Father to earthly parents
Jesus said, "How much more will your Father in heaven give the Holy Spirit
to those who ask him!"

The Holy Spirit is the Father's crowning gift. He is promised to all who ask
the Father for him and who keep on asking. The word for "ask" in this verse
literally means "keep on asking." What askers receive is not just the person
of the Spirit but all the "good gifts" that the Spirit brings into our lives (Matt.
7:11). The Holy Spirit is the all-comprehensive gift, the Gift of all gifts.

There is no more important prayer of the believer than the prayer for the
Holy Spirit. He is the source of every spiritual blessing. Through the Spirit
Jesus lives in us. Through him we receive new hearts, holiness, knowledge,
power, wisdom, and assurance. He produces the fruit of the Spirit in our lives:
"love, joy, peace, patience, kindness, goodness, faithfulness, gentleness and
self-control" (Gal. 5:22-23). He writes the law of God in our hearts so that
we know and want to do what's right (Eze. 36:27). He is the One called to our
side to guide and counsel us (John 14:26). What a remarkably simple way God
works—one gift, many blessings.

When we ask for the Spirit we are not asking for something; we are asking
for someone. We are asking the Father to send a person—the thinking, feeling, willing, acting, talking, listening Third Person of the Holy Trinity. When
he comes, as promised, he comes with all his quickening power, with his infi-

nite wisdom and understanding, with unlimited love and grace, and with his keen awareness of all the realities of our lives.

The presence and power of this person—the Holy Spirit of God—is ours for the asking. There is no way that the Father will withhold the very thing he wants us to have. But we do have to ask. He does not give without our asking. James reminded some prayerless Christians: "You do not have, because you do not ask God" (James 4:2). Andrew Murray challenges us to make asking for the Spirit a priority: "The one thing which, above all others, men and women ought everywhere to ask for . . . is to be filled with the Spirit of God" (*The Full Blessing of Pentecost*, p. 7).

To ask the Father for the Holy Spirit is to ask that the Spirit will fill us, that he will come and take control of every part of our lives. But we need to ask sincerely. Sincere asking means that we really want what the Spirit gives—purity, godliness, holiness, faith-sharing ability, and so on.

If you do not have the Spirit in your life in the fullness that God intends it is not because God is reluctant. He is more than willing. The question is, are you as willing to have the Spirit as the Father is eager to give him to you?

Something to **Think** About
- Do you regularly ask for the Holy Spirit? Why or why not? Why do you think the Father wants you to ask?
- How do you suppose that the Spirit—a thinking, feeling, willing, active person—wants to affect your thoughts, feelings, decisions, and activities?

Something to **Pray** About
- *Praise* the Holy Spirit as the One through whom the Father gives all good gifts.
- *Thank* the Father for the promised gift of the Holy Spirit.
- *Confess* if you have not asked for the Spirit's help or have taken him for granted.
- *Ask* the Father for the Holy Spirit over and over again.
- Tell the Holy Spirit that you willing to *submit* to his control.

Something to **Act On**
Compare Jesus' words in Luke 11:13 to Matthew 7:11. Note the difference. Write out Luke 11:13 on a card. Post it where you will see it every day. Memorize it and claim the promise of the Father in prayer every day.

Praying *with* the Triune God

In the same way, the Spirit helps us in our weakness. We do not know what we ought to pray for, but the Spirit himself intercedes for us with groans that words cannot express. And he who searches our hearts knows the mind of the Spirit, because the Spirit intercedes for the saints in accordance with God's will.

ROMANS 8:26-27

It's one thing to pray *to* the Father, *through* the Son, and *by* Holy Spirit, but it's another thing to find that all three members of the Trinity are involved with us when we pray. Prayer can be perceived as a cycle in which the *Father* initiates prayer; the *Spirit* brings the Father's prayer thoughts to us; and the *Son* brings them back from the believer to the Father's throne.

Writing in *The Arena of Prayer* (p. 32), Ben Jennings helps us visualize the interrelated prayer activity of the Father, the Son, the Holy Spirit, and the believer in the form of a cycle.

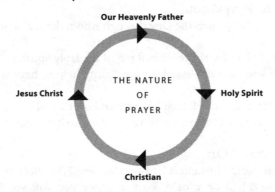

All prayer begins with the *Father*. Prayer flows from him. In Romans 11:36 Paul says of God the Father, "From him ... are all things." That includes prayer. The Father knows what believers ought to pray for. He initiates the prayer cycle so that, through the Spirit, his thoughts on prayer may reach us.

The *Spirit*, who intercedes for us with the Father, does so in order to secure from the Father what we need in order to pray effectively. He then transmits to us the longings or "groanings" of the Father so that we prayer-weak Christians may know what to pray for. The Spirit is the Father's link to us. Paul tells us that the Spirit "searches . . . the deep things of God" and "knows the thoughts of God" (1 Cor. 2:10-11). The Spirit, who always knows God's thoughts, also dwells in us and is able to influence our thoughts. He takes prayer thoughts from heaven to earth. In other words, he carries out his praying in our hearts.

Believers, at the 6 o'clock position on the prayer cycle, aided by the Spirit, become active participants in the prayer cycle. When we "hear" the Holy Spirit and feel the yearnings of God instilled in our hearts by the Spirit we know what to pray for.

Jesus Christ—the one who "who searches hearts and minds" (see Rev. 2:23)—hears our prayers or discerns our unspoken prayers and carries them back to the Father's throne. The Father recognizes them as prayers that originally started with him. Our prayers coming full circle become the means that cause God's will to be accomplished on earth.

Here's how Ben Jennings describes this cycle: "God the Father unfolds His redemptive plan for the world. God the Holy Spirit receives each part of that plan as an intense longing or 'groaning.' He communicates these longings to poorly praying Christians and helps them to pray better. God, the searching Son, receives those longings in the prayers of His people. The Son, the Lord Jesus, then presents those prayers back to the Father and sees that they get answered" (*The Arena of Prayer,* p. 33).

What an awesome arrangement—God getting his work done on earth through our prayers. What a wonderful privilege to be teamed in prayer with the Triune God.

Something to **Think** About
◆ Why do you think God chooses to involve us and our prayers in accomplishing his will in the world?
◆ What could cause this cycle to fail to function as it should?

Something to **Pray** About
◆ *Praise* the Father, the Son, and the Holy Spirit for their part in the cycle of prayer.
◆ *Thank* God for the privilege of being on his "prayer team."
◆ *Confess* any failure you experience as a member of God's "prayer team."
◆ *Ask* the Holy Spirit to help you know what to pray for.

Something to **Act** On
Before you make requests of God, ask him what *he* wants you to pray for in each case. Then pause to listen for the Spirit's prompt. Pray as the Spirit directs.

WEEK THREE

HEARING GOD IN PRAYER

Does God Still Speak Today?

Whether you turn to the right or to the left, your ears will hear a voice behind you, saying, "This is the way; walk in it."
ISAIAH 30:21

My sheep listen to my voice; I know them, and they follow me.
JOHN 10:27

God is a talker. He has always been a talker. This idea is basic to the Christian faith. If God had remained silent we would have no way of knowing him at all. If God is now silent we have no way of relating to him day by day.

We know that he speaks to us in and through his Word—the Bible. But, the question still remains: Does he speak to us today through his Spirit in the way he spoke to men and women of Bible times?

The answer is "yes"! God has a voice; and his sheep hear his voice. Hearing his voice means that a thought, a word, an insight, or an image comes to us from beyond and we perceive that it is from God. What we experience is similar to our own inner self-talk, except that is not self-talk, it is the "Spirit . . . of revelation" talking to us (Eph. 1:17). It's as if God is talking directly to our minds.

When Jesus said "my sheep listen to my voice" he used a word for listen that literally means "constantly listen to the sound of." It was his way of saying that he, the Good Shepherd, would always be there to guide us by speaking to us, and that we would be able to hear his voice and follow him.

God has promised to guide us. The Word of God says: "In all your ways acknowledge him, and he will make your paths straight" (Prov. 3:6). How does he guide us? Sometimes it's as if a voice behind us simply says, "This is the way; walk in it." Believers, who know God, know that it is his voice and accept it as his guidance.

God is a living personal being. He wants a personal relationship with us; a love relationship. The apostle John knew what it meant to have this kind of relationship with God. He said, "Our fellowship is with the Father and with his Son, Jesus Christ" (1 John 1:3); and he wants us to be part of the same relationship. David Watson puts it this way: "God did not finish speaking to us when the scriptures were completed. . . . God is the living God, the God of today; and every day he wants us to enjoy a living relationship with him, involving a two-way conversation" (*Discipleship*, p. 149).

When tempted by Satan to turn bread into stones Jesus' response was, "It is written: 'Man does not live on bread alone, but on every word that comes from the mouth of God'" (Matt. 4:4). The word for "word" in the original language of this passage means a specific word or utterance from God, the kind of utterance that happens in relationship. By such a word, whether from reading the Bible or a thought guided by the Spirit, a believer is able to live in a close and intimate relationship with God.

Jesus knew better than any person who ever lived what it was to hear the Father's voice. He said, "I judge only as I hear" (John 5:30). Hearing from the Father was the basis of his teaching ministry. He said, "My teaching . . . comes from him who sent me" and "I . . . speak just what the Father has taught me" (John 7:16, 8:28). Jesus listened carefully and constantly. He said, "Whatever I say is just what the Father has told me to say" (John 12:50). *Jesus was a listener!* He now lives in us. Through him we can "hear" the Father as he did.

God is not silent. He still speaks today; and since he does, we must listen.

Something to **Think** About

◆ Why did the Father want Jesus to hear him? Why might he want you to hear his voice?

◆ How do you think God feels when we don't take the time or put forth the effort to listen to him?

Something to **Pray** About

◆ *Thank* God for revealing himself through his Word and by his Spirit—the Spirit of revelation (Eph. 1:17).

◆ *Confess* if you have insulted God by failing to listen to what he wants to say to you.

◆ *Ask* God for an "ear to hear" (Rev. 2:7). *Ask* him to teach you how to listen better.

◆ Make a *commitment* to pray what he gives you to pray and to do whatever he tells you to do.

Something to **Act** On

Learn to spend time each day quietly listening for God's voice. Invite him to bring thoughts to your mind from his Word or through his Spirit. Test what you "hear" by the written Word of God.

How Does God Speak Today?

All Scripture is God-breathed and is useful for teaching, rebuking, correcting and training in righteousness, so that all God's people may be thoroughly equipped for every good work.
2 TIMOTHY 3:16-17 (TNIV)

The Spirit himself testifies with our spirit that we are God's children.
ROMANS 8:16

God, being God, is free to speak to us in any way that he chooses. The prophet Joel predicted that a day would come when God would speak through prophecy, visions, dreams, wonders in the heavens, and signs on the earth (Joel 2:28-32). Peter quoted Joel's words to explain what was happening at Pentecost (Acts 2:16ff). Biblical scholars identify up to 30 different ways that God has spoken in the past. Three of the most important ways God speaks today are: the Scriptures, the Spirit's inner testimony, and circumstances. Let's look briefly at each of these.

The primary way that God speaks to us today is clearly through the *Bible*. The psalmist writes: "Your word is a lamp to my feet and a light for my path" (119:105). The apostle Paul reminds us that the God-breathed Scriptures are "useful for teaching, rebuking, correcting and training in righteousness, so that all God's people may be thoroughly equipped for every good work" (2 Tim. 3:16-17, TNIV). It would be foolish for anyone to seek to hear God's voice and neglect the Word of God. The Bible is the surest and best and safest place to hear God speak. We can experience the living reality of God and have fellowship with him by hearing his word personally through the Scriptures. Wise Christians will fill their minds with words from the Word.

But let me caution you! It is possible however to read, study, and memorize the Scriptures and never hear the voice of God. Jesus took issue with Jewish leaders who had diligently studied the Scriptures all their lives—the Scriptures that testified of Christ—but had never seen him there (John 5:37-40). In other words they had never really heard God speak from the pages of holy writ. There is a difference between absorbing knowledge about God and actually hearing him speak. Don't assume that simply reading the Bible is listening to God speak.

A second way that God speaks today is through his Spirit *in our spirits*. In Romans 8:16 Paul writes, "The Spirit himself testifies with our spirit that we are God's children." This communication takes place apart from written revelation. There are no words involved in the Spirit's testimony. He isn't speaking to our minds or giving us thoughts. This is Spirit-to-spirit communication. The truth that we are God's children is transmitted by the person of the Holy Spirit directly and immediately to our spirits. The Spirit's witness gives us an inner awareness and assurance that we are God's children and belong to his family.

A third way that God speaks to us is through *circumstances*. Many of the events in our lives seem to be nothing more than a set of random occurrences. The truth is however that God, who governs the world in accord with his plans and purposes, also controls our lives and often uses circumstances to teach and guide us. If we view and interpret the circumstances of our lives, guided by the Spirit and the Word of God, we will often see and understand God and his ways with us. In other words, God speaks to us through circumstances.

It's important for us to know the ways that God still speaks today. But, what is far more important is to be so tuned in to God that we really hear his voice when he speaks and respond with our heart full of love.

Something to **Think** About
- Why do you suppose God chooses to speak to us in several different ways?
- Can you think of times when God spoke to you personally through the Scriptures? By his Spirit to your spirit? Through circumstances?

Something to **Pray** About
- *Praise* God for revealing himself to you so that you can know him, love him, and trust him.
- *Thank* him for all the ways he has made himself known to you including the Bible, the Spirit's testimony in your heart, and circumstances.
- *Confess* any patterns in your life that have kept you from hearing God.
- *Ask* the Spirit to give you ongoing confirmation in your spirit that you are Abba's child (Rom. 8:15; Gal. 4:6).

Something to **Act** On
Whenever you read the Bible begin with a prayer that you will actually be able to "hear" God speak to you personally.

The Benefits of Hearing God

Trust in the Lord with all your heart and lean not on your own understanding; in all your ways acknowledge him, and he will make your paths straight.

PROVERBS 3:5-6

It is written in the Prophets: "They will be taught by God." Everyone who listens to the Father and learns from him comes to me.

JOHN 6:45

To hear God's voice is to be drawn to him. But hearing him can also be a very practical experience related to the "ordinaries" of daily human life. God is very much in touch with the mundane realities of our lives and wants to help us with them.

Practically speaking, God has promised to guide us if we but listen. He tells us not to lean on our own understanding but to acknowledge him in all our ways. If you do, he says he "will make your paths straight" (Prov. 3:6). God pays attention to the details of our lives. He wants to guide because he knows what is best for us in any and every situation. He can make far more of our lives than we can make of them alone.

Things can go very wrong if we fail to listen. Before moving the ark of the covenant David failed to ask God how it was to be done. Uzzah paid the price with his life. Later David realized the mistake he had made and wrote, "We did not inquire of him about how to do it" (1 Chr. 15:13). As Joshua and the leaders of Israel took possession of the promised land they signed a covenant with the Gibeonites—a regrettable mistake. Coming to grips with their mistake they acknowledged that they "did not inquire of the Lord" (Josh. 9:14).

Things will go right if we listen. When David inquired of the Lord, listened to his response, and executed the detailed battle plans God gave him, he won great victories over his enemies (2 Sam. 5:17-25). That things go right when we listen, however, doesn't always mean that they are easy. When Jesus discerned and submitted to the Father's will in Gethsemane it surely wasn't easy. It took him to the cross. But it was right; and it led to the defeat of Satan, the salvation of world, and the glory of his name.

More important than anything else, listening leads us to Christ himself.

Jesus said, "Everyone who listens to the Father and learns from him comes to me" (John 6:45). When the Father speaks he directs us to his Son because all the answers to life's questions are found in him. The Father has placed his Son Jesus Christ at the center of history and at the center of life. In the words of S. M. Lockridge: "He (Christ) can satisfy all our needs. . . . He supplies strength for the weak. He's available for the tempted and tried; He sympathizes and He sees. He guards and He guides. He heals the sick. . . . He forgives sinners. He discharges debtors; He delivers the captives. He defends the feeble; He blesses the young. . . . He beautifies the meek. . . . He's the key to knowledge. He's the wellspring of wisdom. He's the doorway of deliverance. He's the pathway of peace. He's the roadway to righteousness. He's the highway to holiness. He's the gateway to glory. You can trust Him!" All that he has to give us is ours when we come to him in faith.

The greatest benefit of listening to God is to be found in this—that we are directed by the Father to the Son and to the life he gives. Without his leading life is impossible. With his leading life is full and meaningful. You can't ask for more than that!

Something to **Think** About
+ Where in the mundane realities of your life could you use a good dose of divine wisdom?
+ What things have gone wrong for you because you did not listen to God? What things have gone right because you did listen?

Something to **Pray** About
+ *Praise* the Lord as the totally trustworthy God.
+ *Thank* the Father for leading you to his Son, Jesus Christ—the source of all good.
+ *Confess* any inclination in your heart to "lean on your own understanding" instead of trusting in the Lord.
+ *Ask* God to give you a keen sense of your need for his guidance and the ability to hear his voice.

Something to **Act** On
Think ahead to one decision you have to make in the next few days or weeks. Ask God to guide you in that decision. Spend time listening and ask him to reveal his will to you.

Is That Really You God?

The man who enters by the gate is the shepherd of his sheep. The watch-man opens the gate for him, and the sheep listen to his voice. He calls his own sheep by name and leads them out. When he has brought out all his own, he goes on ahead of them, and his sheep follow him because they know his voice. But they will never follow a stranger; in fact, they will run away from him because they do not recognize a stranger's voice.
JOHN 10:2-5

The biggest problem in hearing God's voice is knowing for sure that it is really *his* voice that we hear. Is it possible, we may ask, that what I think I hear is really self-talk? Could it be just my imagination? Are there other voices that attempt to masquerade as his voice?

The answer to these questions is found in Jesus' words. Sheep, he says, "listen to [the shepherd's] voice . . . his sheep follow him because they know his voice . . . they will never follow a stranger . . . because they do not recognize his voice" (John 10:2-5). Jesus is the Shepherd. Believers are the sheep. Believers will listen to and recognize the voice of the Shepherd. They will also know that certain voices are not his and will flee from them.

The better we know the Shepherd the more certain we will be of his voice. To get to know him we have to spend time with him. The more time that we spend with him the better we will know him.

The Shepherd knows us well. Because he knows our names, our thoughts, our feelings, our hopes, and our ambitions he is able to relate to us personally. As we come to know *his* name, *his* thoughts, *his* ways, and *his* will we will also come to know what his voice sounds like.

There are four possible voices that we can "hear": the voice of the devil, the voice of the world, the voice of sinful flesh, and the voice of the Lord. Be sure when listening that the voice you hear is God's voice and not the others. If I am uncertain about a voice I hear then I need to ask God to silence the other voices: to squelch voice of the devil, to shut down the voice of the world, and to tune out the voice of sinful flesh. That's a prayer that God always answers. He is eager to protect us from the lies and deceits of other voices. He clears the channels of our hearts so that we hear only his voice.

It is also important to test what you think God may be saying by his nature and his Word and, if necessary, by godly counselors. Ask yourself, "Is this the kind of thing God would say? Does it fit with his Word? Do godly counselors confirm that it is probably a word from the Lord?" If doubt remains ask God to further confirm his word to you and give you assurance that it is really he who is speaking. I find that he is usually willing to do that. He wants us to hear his voice and to be sure of it.

In all of this it's important to remember that the main reason God speaks to us is not simply to guide us. Guidance is only a part of a life lived in loving fellowship with God. Listening is mostly about love—his love for us and our love for him. God, above all, wants you to "hear" his heartbeat, a heart that beats with love. If you listen hard, it's hard to miss!

Something to **Think** About
◆ When have you heard the voice of the Shepherd? What do you remember about what you heard?
◆ When have the other voices—the devil, the world, or the sinful nature—tried to get your attention? What did you do with them? Why?

Something to **Pray** About
◆ *Praise* the Good Shepherd for his good shepherding.
◆ *Thank* him for guiding you, protecting you, and keeping you from harm.
◆ If you have listened to the other voices and followed their leadings, *confess* that to your Shepherd and ask his forgiveness.
◆ *Ask* your Shepherd to help you hear his voice, to follow his lead, and to spurn those who would lead in wrong ways.

Something to **Act** On
Read and meditate on Psalm 23. Thank the Shepherd for everything he does for you as mentioned in the psalm. Try to translate the metaphors of the ancient shepherding world into current situations in your life.

Learning How to Listen

Mary . . . sat at the Lord's feet listening to what he said. . . . Only one thing is needed. Mary has chosen what is better, and it will not be taken away from her.
LUKE 10:39, 42

He who has an ear, let him hear what the Spirit says to the churches.
REVELATION 2:7

Learning to hear God is not a matter of discovering a formula. There are no surefire techniques. God is a person. Learning to hear him is a matter of being attentive to a real person. In other words, to improve our hearing we need to improve our relationship.

Listening to God is not a skill that we inherently possess. It has to be learned in the same way that a growing child learns to listen to her mother's voice. There are going to be mistakes. God will be patient, more patient than any parent, as we live and learn. Following are several suggested activities that will help you learn how to listen.

First, *turn your mind toward God* intentionally and often. Get oriented to his ways of thinking and acting. Create times, like Mary, to sit quietly at the feet of Jesus and pay close attention to what he is saying. Be alert to what is happening in your life, to thoughts that are surfacing in your mind and to the stirrings of your heart. Is God in these things? Talk to him about them. He is interested in every event, every thought, and every stirring. He wants *in* on your life just as much as you want *in* on his thoughts.

Second, *ask God for a listening ear*. That's a prayer he will not refuse. Ask him to reveal himself to you and to train you to hear his voice. He is a great teacher. Invite him to interrupt you with *his* thoughts about any issue or situation. Ask him to impress upon you situations and people that you should pray for. Ask him to guide you to assignments that he wants you to carry out for him. God loves that kind of asking.

Third, *position yourself to hear*. Meditate on the Word of God day and night. Hide the Word in your heart so that God can draw upon it at will. Be silent often enough and long enough to give him an opportunity to speak to your heart. Ask God questions that will invite his response, questions like: "Is there a sin I need to deal with?" or "How can I be more fruitful for you?" Then wait for his answer.

Fourth, *trust God to speak.* It's his responsibility. Don't try to force him. You can't anyway; but you don't have to. He wants to communicate with his children. He told us he would. He will speak in ways that he chooses: through the Scriptures, by arranging circumstances, through trusted counselors, and by an inner voice. How he speaks is his responsibility; expecting him to speak and being prepared to listen is ours.

Fifth, *be ready to respond.* God is not in the business of revealing himself to us so that we can decide whether we will respond. Don't expect him to speak at all unless you are committed to responding. His word may call for confession. His guidance may lead to action. His Spirit may lead you to pray for or reach out to someone you know. He may simply want you to say "thank you."

Learn to listen and you will find yourself on an incredible journey to a closer walk with God and a joy greater than you can imagine.

Something to **Think** About
- How often do you, like Mary, take time to be with Jesus and pay close attention to him? When might you take that kind of time for him?
- Have you ever asked God for a "listening" ear? Is that something you really want? What would it require of you?

Something to **Pray** About
- *Praise* the Spirit who still speaks to churches and Christians.
- *Thank* God that you have the ability to "hear" his voice and that he stands ready to help you learn how to do it.
- If you have been an "anxious-about-many-things Martha" instead of an "at-the-feet-of-Jesus Mary" you may have something to *confess.*
- *Ask* the Lord to give you a responsive heart and the willingness to do his will as he reveals it to you no matter what.

Something to **Act** On
Ask God three questions:
- What am I doing that you do not approve of?
- What am I not doing that you want me to do?
- What am I doing that you want more of?

Write down the answers he brings to your mind and then act on what he tells you.

Week Four

PRAYING JESUS' WAY

Praying Like a Child

This, then, is how you should pray: "Our Father in heaven. . . ."
Matthew 6:9

How great is the love the Father has lavished on us, that we should be called children of God! And that is what we are!
1 John 3:1

To pray to the Father in heaven is to pray like a child. When Jesus taught us pray, "Our Father," he was teaching us to pray as children. The words "Our Father" are more than a way to address God. They involve us in a relationship—a Father/child love relationship. That's the kind of relationship John had in mind when he said, "How great is the love the Father has lavished on us, that we should be called children of God! And that is what we are!"

Jesus was the first person on earth ever to call God his Father. No Old Testament prophet, priest, or king ever dared to address God in that way. Already as a young boy Jesus shocked his parents with the question: "Didn't you know I had to be in my Father's house?" Jesus put this unique Father/child relationship on display throughout his earthly days. John's gospel records Jesus using the term Father at least 118 times, 13 of these as he speaks to his Father in prayer.

You and I are invited into the same privileged relationship that Jesus had with his heavenly Father. Jesus did everything necessary to remove the sin that made such a relationship impossible and has now given us "the right to become children of God" (John 1:12). Dennis Fuque makes the point: "The closest, most meaningful, important and significant relationship in the entire universe is between the Father and the Son. This is the relationship we, as His children, have been invited into" (*The Lord's Prayer as Real Prayer*, prepublication manuscript, p. 28).

Knowing that God is our Father means that he is easily approachable. We can come to him as comfortably as a small child comes to his or her daddy. We can approach him simply, directly, and confidently without pretense or pomposity. And we come knowing that he is ready to hear us and to listen to our prayers with tender sympathy and patience.

This does not mean that we can treat him with a casual chumminess that brings him down to our level. We must forever remember that he is "Our Father *in heaven*." He can be approached by his children comfortably but not mechanically. His tender love is combined with awesome power. His power and love work together in such a way that his love is backed by power, his power is directed by his love. In his love he draws near; in his might he remains transcendent.

The prayer words that Jesus puts in our mouth settle one more thing. They settle our relationship to our brothers and sisters in Christ. Jesus does not teach us to say "my Father" but "our Father." There is not an "I," "me," "my," or "mine" in the whole Lord's Prayer. We are all part of the Father's very large family made up of believers from other neighborhoods, other churches, other nations, and other cultures. To say "Our Father" is to remember that we walk with and pray with millions of other children of God whom the Father also hears with tender sympathy.

The prayer words, "Our Father," are not for everyone. God does not *become* a Father to those who simply pray these words. We are able to pray these words only if we have become his children by receiving Jesus Christ and believing in his name (John 1:12). To all such he gives the right to become children of God, to know him and speak to him as Father.

Something to **Think** About

♦ Why did Jesus teach us to address God as Father and not Almighty God, Lord of Heaven, Great King, or some other such title?

♦ What does it mean to you to know that God is your heavenly Father?

Something to **Pray** About

♦ *Praise* God as your Father, the most wonderful Father the world has ever known.

♦ *Thank* him for giving you the right to become one of his children.

♦ *Confess* any unchildlike behavior you are aware of.

♦ *Ask* for a strong and growing love relationship with your Father in heaven.

Something to **Act** On

Practice starting your prayers by address God as Father. Then pause for ten seconds or so to let his "Fatherness" sink in before you go on.

Praying for the Father's Glory

I will do whatever you ask in my name, so that the Son may bring glory to the Father. You may ask me for anything in my name, and I will do it.
                                    JOHN 14:13-14

I have brought you glory on earth by completing the work you gave me to do.
                                    JOHN 17:4

The best way for us to be sure that God will answer our prayers of supplication is to ask the question: "If God grants my request, who will get the glory?" If the answer is clearly "God will," then we can expect to receive what we have asked. If the answer is "I will," then we should not expect to receive what we ask for. If it is not for God's glory, Jesus isn't going to do it.

There was a time when Jesus' disciples were not certain that they would be able to carry on the ministry that he was passing on to them. Jesus assured them that they could. He gave as the reason for his reassuring answer: "I will do whatever you ask in my name, so that the Son may bring glory to the Father." In saying this Jesus was telling them not only *that* he would answer their prayers; he was telling them *how* they should pray. He was saying something like, "If your prayers are for the Father's glory then you will get what you ask for."

The Father's glory was the keynote of Jesus' entire life on earth. It was his first thought in every situation and his highest motivation. Near the end of his life he could say to the Father, "I have brought you glory on earth by completing the work you gave me to do." The Father's glory is still the keynote of his life as from his heavenly throne he hears and answers the prayers of his people. So when you and I ask anything that is for the Father's glory he promises to answer with a "yes"!

I am certain that Jesus not only agrees to hear and answer such prayers, but that he is eager to have us pray many prayers of this type. To make requests that will bring glory to the Father is to bless the heart of Jesus and to join hands with him in achieving his greatest desire. To pray selfish prayers, intended for personal glory, is an offense to Christ. For the sake of God's glory, let us pray rightly and let us pray much.

The glory of God is meant to be the prime motive in all that we do. You were chosen, says Paul, "for the praise of his glory" (Eph. 1: 12). Speak and serve, says Peter, "so that in all things God may be praised" (1 Peter 4:11). Whatever you do, God's Word reminds us, "do it all for the glory of God" (1 Cor. 10:31). His glory should be the prime motive when we intercede. If we truly are living for God's glory then it will be natural for us to pray in a way that gives God the glory.

All prayer is meant to glorify God. Heartfelt *praise* and *thanksgiving* glorify him directly. Sincere *confession* glorifies him by acknowledging his standards as right. Prayers of humble *submission* clearly honor his will and his lordship. It's when praying prayers of *petition* and *intercession* that we need to be the most careful to discern what would bring him glory. And, if we are not certain how to pray, we can still pray with the assurance that Jesus will answer in a way that will bring glory to God.

Maybe we should start our prayers of intercession by humbly asking, "Lord, help me to know what would bring you the most glory" and then frame our prayers based on what we hear. God's heart will be wide open to such prayers.

Something to **Think** About

- How does Jesus' commitment to glorify the Father in all things affect the way he answers our prayers?
- What kinds of prayer requests will give Christ opportunity to answer in a way that will glorify the Father?

Something to **Pray** About

- *Praise* Jesus for his Father-glorifying life.
- *Thank* Jesus for his commitment to answer your prayers in ways that glorify the Father.
- If you are aware of having prayed thoughtless, self-glorifying prayers, *confess* that to the Lord as wrong.
- *Ask* Jesus to help you always be conscious of the Father's glory when you pray.

Something to **Act** On

As you make prayer requests to God practice asking yourself, "If God grants this request will he get the glory?"

Prayer: Opening the Floodgates of Grace

Ask and it will be given you; seek and you will find; knock and the door will be opened to you. For everyone who asks receives; he who seeks finds; and to him who knocks, the door will be opened. . . . How much more will your Father in heaven give good gifts to those who ask him!
MATTHEW 7:7-8, 11

Floodgates are adjustable gates that control water flow in a reservoir system. My mental image of floodgates comes from an area of California where water turned deserts into fruitful farmland. The water came from reservoirs in the mountains. When the floodgates were opened water poured through them filling the irrigation canals, flowing out through ditches and trenches, and saturating the roots of every fruit tree and every grapevine in that irrigation district with life-giving moisture.

When Jesus said, "Ask and it will be given you; seek and you will find; knock and the door will be opened to you" he was challenging us to ask, and seek, and knock so that the floodgates of the Father's "good gifts" would open for us. No need to wonder what these gifts are. They are "everything we need for life and godliness" (2 Peter 1:3), gifts like faith, hope, love, joy, peace, mercy, patience, kindness, goodness, faithfulness, gentleness, self-control, knowledge, wisdom, understanding, strength, holiness, righteousness, godliness, purity, humility, and so on. Can you imagine what your life in Christ would be like if you had a fresh supply of these gifts every day? Jesus could. That's why he "set us up" to ask for and receive them constantly.

The good gifts Jesus promises are free; they are of grace. We can't earn them, but we don't have to. All we have to do is ask for them and they are ours. Imagine yourself walking into your favorite supermarket. A man stops you at the door and says: "Congratulations! You are our ten thousandth customer. Your groceries won't cost you anything today. Everything you can get in your cart will be free." Wouldn't you abandon your limited shopping list and fill your cart with all the best things you could find to fit in it? That's what Jesus wants us to do with his offer of spiritual riches.

To grasp the import of Jesus' message in these words we must understand that he is telling us to pray this way *for ourselves*. We cannot claim this promise when we are interceding for others. Their hearts and lives may hinder the reception of the gift. But if we seriously desire these spiritual riches for ourselves then we will ask with the faith and obedience that are necessary, and the floodgates will be opened for us.

Jesus so wants us to have these graces that he doesn't just recommend that we ask; he commands it. The verbs for ask, and seek, and knock are in the imperative. We *must* ask and seek and knock. If we don't we are being disobedient and will pay the price. Jesus commands this, not to lay another burden on our backs, but so that we won't miss the blessing.

Jesus also expects us to be persistent in asking. It's not as if he is offering us an emergency system—a spiritual 911 number—that we can use in a crisis. Jesus wants us to use it all the time, every day; not just in emergencies. The verbs literally mean "*keep on* asking, *keep on* seeking, and *keep on* knocking." The persistence is necessary not because God is a reluctant giver, but because our need is great and constant, and he chooses to give in response to our continued asking.

The Father is ready to open the floodgates of grace for you. Do you want him to? If so, then ask and seek and knock—and he will!

Something to **Think** About

◆ Why does Jesus want us to ask in order to receive his "good gifts?" Why doesn't he just give them?

◆ Which of the 21 "grace gifts" mentioned in the second paragraph would most like to have today?

Something to **Pray** About

◆ *Praise* God, the gracious giver of all good gifts.

◆ *Thank* him that all his good gifts are free to believers for the asking.

◆ *Ask* God to open the floodgates of his grace for you.

◆ If you have presumed on God by thinking he gives automatically without your asking, *confess* that to him.

◆ In response to God's command for you to ask, seek, and knock, make a *commitment* to do that regularly.

Something to **Act** On

Thoughtfully ask God for each of the 21 gifts mentioned in the second paragraph. Pause as you mention each one and think about what it means to receive that gift. Thank God for the gift immediately knowing that God will most certainly give it.

The Master Key of Prayer

If you remain in me and my words remain in you, ask whatever you wish, and it will be given you.

JOHN 15:7

Prayer is a relationship—a love relationship with the Father, the Son, and the Holy Spirit. What prayer becomes in our lives depends on what is happening in that relationship. A good relationship with Jesus is the prime factor in receiving what we ask for. If our relationship with Christ can truly be defined as "remaining in him and his words remaining in us" then, says Jesus, you can "ask whatever you wish, and it will be given you."

Imagine for a moment that you were the son or daughter of a king. Destined to inherit his throne you were, at a very young age, taken into the court to live and work alongside your father. You observed him, listened to him, and learned from him. You shared in his thoughts, his feelings, his decisions, and his activities. You embraced his goals, his vision, and his passions. You loved your father deeply and he loved you. You were very close. You had a very special bond. Nobody that knew you could miss the fact that you and your father were very much alike.

When you came of age your father sent you out into his kingdom to represent him. Even though you were apart you kept up the relationship. Couriers kept the messages flowing between the two of you. When you dealt with problems, needed funds, or required help your father always gave you whatever you asked for. He knew you. He trusted you. And when he sent directives or asked for your help, you always did what he asked without question. You respected him. You trusted him. You had this bond between the two of you.

Now transfer that image to another King, Jesus, who reigns in heaven today. You are his child. You know him; you have listened to him and learned from him. You share his thoughts, his feelings, his decisions, and his activities. You embrace his goals and his vision for the kingdom. You have a special bond with him, a bond that the Bible calls "remaining in him."

By means of prayer you keep up communication with him. When he gives directions or asks your help you always do what he asks. His "words remain in you." When you need his help he always grants what you ask. You are his trusted representative, building his kingdom here on earth. You can "ask whatever you wish, and it will be given you."

This is not just a mental picture. This is reality. We are Christ's representatives. He is building his kingdom here on earth. The Father always hears Christ. And so, if we remain in him and his words remain in us, God will always hear us for the same reason he always hears his Son. It cannot be any other way.

To "remain" in Christ means to be bonded with him in a life-giving relationship like that between a vine and a branch. It means that we think like him, feel like him, and act like him because his words are in us. It means that we pray like him and ask for the very things he would be asking for if he were in our place.

The master key of prayer, then, is the love relationship we have with God. His love for us, expressed through Christ's "remaining in us," transforms us. The prayers that flow out of our transformed hearts become an expression of our love for God and of our desire to bless his name and build his kingdom. Such prayers always please God and evoke from him the promised "yes" answer.

Something to **Think** About

◆ What will make Jesus willing to give you whatever you ask?
◆ If Jesus' words remain in you what will your life be like?

Something to **Pray** About

◆ *Praise* Jesus for his power—the power that answers your prayers.
◆ *Thank* him for this incredible promise that stands at the heart of prayer.
◆ *Confess* anything that may be shaping your life other than the words of Christ implanted in your heart.
◆ *Ask* the Holy Spirit to bind you to Christ and to download the words of Christ into your heart.

Something to **Act** On

Read John 15:1-8, 15-16. Underline every use of the word "fruit" and "fruitful" in these verses. What is the link between fruit and "remaining in Christ?" Between fruit and prayer? Between fruit and the Father's glory?

Prayer for Harvest Workers

*When [Jesus] saw the crowds, he had compassion on them, because
they were harassed and helpless, like sheep without a shepherd. Then
he said to his disciples, "The harvest is plentiful but the workers are
few. Ask the Lord of the harvest, therefore, to send out workers into his
harvest field."*
MATTHEW 9:36-38

Despite the fact that Jesus commanded us to pray for workers in the harvest, I seldom hear such prayers in the church today. And, frankly, I
admit that I haven't been very faithful in praying for harvest workers either. I
think that the problem has to do with our way of looking at things. If we saw
people as Jesus sees them and understood prayer as he does we would pray for
harvest workers constantly.

What was Jesus' frame of reference? First, when he saw the crowds of people,
he saw that they were "harassed and helpless" and his heart was moved with
compassion. In other words he was moved at the very depths of his being. It
wasn't just earthly problems like poverty, sickness, injustice, or loneliness that
caused his heart to ache. It was also their hopeless spiritual condition caused
by sin and Satan. He desperately wanted them to have eternal life as well as his
love, his joy, and his peace. If we come to the point of caring for hurting and
helpless people as deeply as Jesus does, then I am sure that we will pray for
harvest workers with more of his compassion.

Second, Jesus knew that the harvest belonged to "the Lord of the harvest"—
his Father. The "sheep without a shepherd" are *his* lost sheep. His heart aches
for them to be found. He has even sent his own Son, the Shepherd of heaven,
to search for them. When they are found and brought back to the fold, there
will be a great celebration in heaven. If our hearts beat with the Shepherd's
heart we will care as he cares, and we will pray as he taught us to pray.

Third, Jesus observed that "the harvest is plentiful." I wonder if we really
believe that today. It surely doesn't seem very plentiful. In fact in many places
today the harvest seems downright sparse. Many who hear the good news
reject it. Others start out well and then fall away. But Christ, who sees in ways
that we do not, sees a bountiful harvest. And he commands us to pray in the

54

faith that there is a harvest and that harvest workers will bring it in.

Fourth, Jesus understood that prayer is the means God has ordained in order to raise up a harvest force and release it into the harvest. To that end he charges us to "ask the Lord of the harvest . . . to send out workers into his harvest field." God will choose and call and equip the workers. But he is moved to do this in response to our prayers. Dare we say that he will not to do this if we do not pray for it? If we really understand that the harvest force depends on our prayers we will surely pray with urgency.

Finally, Jesus' idea of a harvest worker was not what we normally think. We tend to think of pastors, evangelists, and missionaries as God's harvest workers, and they are. But Jesus calls all of us to be harvest workers. The harvest is all around us. We are all empowered by the Spirit to be witnesses for him (Acts 1:8). We are all called to "make disciples of all nations" (Matt. 28:19). So when we pray for harvest workers we are praying that all of God's people, wherever they are, will see the harvests that God has prepared and step up to the task of being the Father's harvest workers.

Would you pray that with me? And, would you also be the answer to your prayers?

Something to **Think** About
- ◆ What evidence is there that the disciples prayed for harvest workers and that the Lord answered?
- ◆ What do you think would happen if your church devoted itself to pray for harvest workers? Be specific.
- ◆ Where do you fit into Jesus' call? Are you a part of the harvest? A harvest worker? An intercessor for harvest workers? All of the above?

Something to **Pray** About
- ◆ *Praise* Jesus for his compassionate concern for lost people.
- ◆ *Thank* him that you are part of the harvest that has come in (assuming that is true).
- ◆ If you seldom pray for harvest workers, *talk to* the Lord about that failure.
- ◆ *Ask* the Lord for harvest workers in your church, your community, your nation, and the world.
- ◆ Make a *commitment* to pray for harvest workers regularly.

Something to **Act** On
If you are part of a prayer group, use Matthew 9:36-38 to challenge members to pray regularly and earnestly for harvest workers. Watch for God's answer.

WEEK FIVE

PRAYER AND
SPIRITUAL WARFARE

Prayer and Spiritual Warfare

I tell you the truth, anyone who has faith in me will do what I have been doing. He will do even greater things than these, because I am going to the Father. And I will do whatever you ask in my name, so that the Son may bring glory to the Father.
John 14:12-14

God anointed Jesus of Nazareth with the Holy Spirit and power, and . . . he went around doing good and healing all who were under the power of the devil, because God was with him.
Acts 10:38

Christ's reason for coming to earth was twofold. He came, Luke tells us, "to seek and to save what was lost" (Luke 19:10). He also came, John tells us, "to destroy the devil's work" (1 John 3:8). These are two sides of the same work. In order to seek and save the lost Jesus had to destroy the devil's work. By destroying the devil's works he saves lost people.

During the days of his ministry on earth Jesus worked havoc on Satan's works. "He went around doing good and healing all who were under the power of the devil" (Acts 10:38). By his death he "[destroyed] him who holds the power of death—that is, the devil—and [freed] those who all their lives were held in slavery by their fear of death" (Heb. 2:14). Paul tells us that he "disarmed the powers and authorities . . . triumphing over them by the cross" (Col. 2:15).

From his heavenly throne Jesus continues to frustrate the work of the devil; only now he does it through believers. To disciples, who questioned how his work could continue after he left, he said, "Anyone who has faith in me will do what I have been doing. He will do even greater things than these." The "things" he had in mind included "destroying the devil's works" and "healing all who were under the power of the devil." This means that believers who continue his work on earth will be engaged in spiritual warfare.

How are we able to do the kind of works Jesus did? Jesus anticipated this question and addressed it in what he said next: "I am going to the Father. And I will do whatever you ask in my name, so that the Son may bring glory to the Father." He was saying, "I will be on the throne. You will be on earth. What you ask in my name I will do. That's how my work will continue." In other words, we ask and Christ acts. Our praying is key to his ongoing work. Through our prayers he continues "doing good and healing all who are under the power of the devil."

True prayer will always pit us against the powers of darkness. When we pray for captives to be set free, we will be praying against the one who holds people in bondage. When we pray for people to know the truth, we will be opposing the father of lies. When we pray that people will see the "light," we will be at odds with the god of this age who blinds the eyes of unbelievers. Christ chooses to continue his saving work and to disarm Satan through our prayers.

Of course it is not our prayers that defeat Satan. Christ defeated Satan once for all on the cross. But he now enforces the victory already won through our prayers. And he will continue to undo the work of the devil through our prayers until the day of Satan's final defeat.

No wonder the devil fears the prayers of God's people so much. He can cope with everything we can humanly muster against him. But he cannot cope with the almighty arm of the Lord that moves through our prayers. His only hope is to keep us from praying. So keep on praying and give the enemy no hope!

Something to **Think** About

◆ What prayers of yours are causing the work of Christ on earth to continue?

◆ What kinds of prayer does the devil hate and fear? What kinds of prayer does he *not* fear? Think this through.

Something to **Pray** About

◆ *Praise* God for the power of the Holy Spirit with whom he anointed Jesus for ministry.

◆ *Thank* Jesus for the "great things" he has done for you and for all who believe in him. Be specific.

◆ If your prayers have been no threat to the devil, ask yourself why and *confess* any sin that you may discover.

◆ *Ask* God for the kind of prayer life that will really threaten Satan.

◆ *Intercede* for persons you know who seem to be caught in Satan's web.

Something to **Act** On

Make a list of prayers that, when answered by God, will undo the devil's work.

Prayer and Spiritual Struggle

For our struggle is not against flesh and blood, but against the rulers, against the authorities, against the powers of this dark world and against the spiritual forces of evil in the heavenly realms. Therefore put on the full armor of God . . . and pray in the Spirit on all occasions with all kinds of prayers and requests. With this in mind, be alert and always keep on praying for all the saints.
EPHESIANS 6:12-13, 18

The New Testament often reminds us that we have a spiritual enemy who is actively seeking to destroy us. That's the bad news. The good news is that, in our struggle with spiritual forces of evil, we have a way to stand and to thwart his efforts to harm us.

The battle is real. Paul states, "Our struggle is not against flesh and blood, but against the rulers, against the authorities, against the powers of this dark world." This struggle is not an easy one. The forces of evil we are dealing with are illusively invisible. We don't read about them in our daily newspapers; we can't legislate against them. Yet, they are real, very real; as real as the people we rub shoulders with every day. And they are dedicated to our destruction. They work at it every day, in every way possible.

Our security in the face of these dreadful powers is to put on God's armor: truth, righteousness, the gospel, faith, salvation, and the word of God (Eph. 6:17). But that's not all. There is one more important thing for us to do and that is to pray.

Prayer is one of the mightiest weapons we have in defeating the devil. Paul is explicit about our use of prayer in the struggle. He says, "With this in mind" (that is, keeping in mind the struggle against the forces of evil) "always keep on praying for all the saints." By prayer we bring down the devil, and by prayer we lift up the saints.

John Piper, writing in *Mission Frontiers*, asks us to imagine the Son coming to us and saying "My Father wants me to extend my mission to you. It's dangerous, but you can't lose; the mission will succeed. He's given me these transmitters here. Each one is tuned to the general's frequency. As long as you stay in battle, fighting His war in His ways, you will always have free access by the transmitter to the general. Go use them, and I'll do whatever you ask for the war cause" (July 1989).

Despite Paul's command and God's wonderful promise the church today is not much engaged in warfare prayer. The problem is, as Piper points out in the same article, that we tend to operate, not as if we are at war, but with a "peacetime casualness." We are but little aware of the dangers that face us. We don't see the spiritual terrorists. We can't imagine the spiritual "roadside bombs" that maim believers. The evening news doesn't carry spiritual casualty statistics. When problems arise our knee-jerk reaction is to look for the "flesh and blood" culprits—exactly what Scripture does not want us to do.

The truth is that we *are* at war, at war with a real and terrible enemy, an enemy that is too formidable for our meager weapons. But fully armored and fully prayed-up soldiers of Christ do not fear. He who is "our strength and our shield" is ever with us.

Christ's desire is for all of us to stand. He has all the power necessary to make us stand. Yet he asks us to be engaged with him through our prayers. "Be alert," he commands, "and always keep on praying for all the saints." Pray that *all* will stand.

Who will stand because you have prayed?"

Something to **Think** About

◆ What do you normally struggle with? What do you find if you look behind the scenes of your struggles?

◆ Do most Christians you know operate with a "peacetime casualness" or with an awareness that we are at war with a ruthless invisible enemy?

Something to **Pray** About

◆ *Praise* Jesus Christ who has dealt the death blow to our mortal enemy.

◆ *Thank* God for the spiritual armor he provides for us and for the protection of prayer.

◆ *Confess* any failure in using the armor and in being alert to "always keep on praying for all the saints."

◆ *Ask* the Spirit to help you pray "on all occasions with all kinds of prayers and requests."

◆ *Intercede* for embattled saints and prodigal sons and daughters. Pray that they will "be strong in the Lord and in his mighty power."

Something to **Act** On

Write the last sentence of Ephesians 6:18 boldly on top of a page. Then list the names of those who need your protective prayers.

Prayer and Spiritual Protection

Bring us not into temptation, but deliver us from the evil one.
MATTHEW 6:13 (ASV)

Holy Father, protect them by the power of your name—the name you gave me—so that they may be one as we are one. . . . My prayer is not that you take them out of the world but that you protect them from the evil one.   JOHN 17:11, 15

Several years ago Bill Bright, founder of Campus Crusade for Christ, formulated a gospel presentation that begins with these words: "God loves you and has a wonderful plan for your life." Sometime later Timothy Warner wrote an article in *Discipleship Journal* entitled: "Satan Hates You and Has a Terrible Plan for Your Life." These two concepts—God's love for us and Satan's hatred for us—represent the opposing poles of spiritual activity in our world today. No one understood these two poles better than Jesus.

Because he understood the reality and power of evil in the world so well Jesus taught us to pray: "Father . . . deliver us from the evil one." It was his way of alerting us to the danger of the devil's schemes and our need for the Father's protection.

Prayer is a form of spiritual protection. Twice Jesus asked the Father to protect his disciples. First he prayed, "Holy Father, protect them by the power of your name", and then a little later, "My prayer is not that you take them out of the world but that you protect them from the evil one." Jesus knew full well the destructive power of the evil one and did the most important thing he could do to protect them. He prayed.

Today we face the same kind of spiritual dangers that the disciples faced. The evil one is anti-Christ, anti-church, and anti-Christian. He is hostile to God and opposes his purposes. He hates us and has a terrible plan for our lives. He is bent on our destruction. It's being aware of this reality that drives us to pray, "Father . . . deliver us from the evil one." No one of us is free from the need for this prayer.

We are no match for the devil. We need the Father's shield of protection over us. It's prayer that brings the Almighty to our defense. He is our sure source of protection.

Not everyone today believes in a real devil. Satan is a great deceiver. He tries to deceive people into believing that he does not exist, then he seeks to work in their lives without hindrance. If that doesn't work he will settle for getting lots of attention. That way he can draw attention away from God and create fear in people's lives. A third deceptive trick of the devil is to get people to laugh at him as an amusing and harmless creature with horns, forked tail, hooves, and carrying a pitchfork. Don't be duped by any one of these. Stay out of danger! Be aware that he is real; don't pass him off as funny; and give your attention to Christ the King who conquered him.

Here are a few suggestions to be assured of the Father's protection. First, humbly realize how unable you are to cope with the devil yourself. Second, ask for the Father's protection with full awareness of the danger inherent in the evil one. Third, trust that the Father will hear and answer your prayer. He loves you and is fully able to protect you. Finally, be ready to obey the Lord in all things. Satan cannot do you any real harm if you are walking obediently in the way of the Lord.

God wants to give you complete victory over his archenemy, the devil. The path to victory begins with a simple prayer: "Father, deliver me from the evil one."

Something to **Think** About

♦ Think of a time when Satan tried to harm you but failed. Think of a time when he succeeded in harming you. What was the difference?
♦ Try to identify some specific ways that the Father protected you in the past? How is he now protecting you?

Something to **Pray** About

♦ *Praise* God for his protective power and his willingness to shield you from spiritual harm.
♦ *Thank* Jesus for his protective prayers in your behalf. He is at the right hand of God interceding for you.
♦ If you have failed to ask for the Father's protection, or failed to pray protective prayers for those near you, *deal with that* before the Lord.
♦ *Ask* God to teach you to pray "deliver us from the evil one" with a keen awareness of real spiritual danger.
♦ *Intercede* for those near you who need the Father's protection.

Something to **Act** On

Identify one or two points at which you are most vulnerable to the evil one. Ask the Father to cover you in these areas.

Prayer and Spiritual Authority

Jesus . . . gave them power and authority to drive out all demons and to cure diseases, and he sent them out to preach. . . .
Luke 9:1

The seventy-two returned with joy and said, "Lord even the demons submit to us in your name." He replied, "I saw Satan fall like lightning from heaven. I have given you authority to trample on snakes and scorpions and to overcome all the power of the enemy. . . ."
Luke 10:17-19

[Jesus'] disciples asked him privately, "Why couldn't we drive [the demon] out?" He replied, "This kind can come out only by prayer."
Mark 9:28-29

Authority is the right to give commands and enforce obedience. Spiritual authority is the right to do this in the spiritual realm. When Jesus was on earth he had this kind of authority. He gave commands to evil spirits, to diseases, and even to forces of nature, and they obeyed his orders.

Jesus made frequent use of his authority to free people from demons and to defeat the powers of darkness. His words and actions often left people flabbergasted. On a trip to Capernaum Jesus dealt decisively with an agitated evil spirit and cast it out of a man. "Be quiet!" he said. "Come out of him." "The people were amazed and said to each other 'What is this teaching? With authority and power he gives orders to evil spirits and they come out'" (Luke 4:36).

Jesus did not, however, keep this authority to himself. He broadened the base of his ministry by delegating spiritual authority to his disciples—first to the twelve and then to 72. Luke tells us that Jesus "gave them power and authority to drive out demons and to cure diseases." After a foray of ministry activities using their newly delegated authority the disciples came back saying joyfully: "Lord even the demons submit to us in your name." Jesus' response was, "I saw Satan fall like lightning from heaven."

Spiritual authority of this type has to be handled correctly. Its proper use depends on a prayerful trusting relationship with the person who has given the authority in the first place. On one occasion when the disciples attempted to use their delegated authority to cast out a demon it didn't work. When Jesus came on the scene he took control of the situation and cast out the demon. Afterward the disciples asked him, "Why couldn't we drive it out?" he replied, "This kind can come out only by prayer." Prayer forges the necessary link between the authority-giver and the authority-user. Without the link there is no authority.

Today Jesus delegates his authority to praying Christians. He invites us to direct his activities on earth through our prayers. Our prayers move his hands. Our prayers bring his healing to hurting people. By our prayers Satan still falls like lightning from heaven. By means of our prayers the kingdom is advanced and God's cause on earth prospers. That is what Christ intended by delegating his spiritual authority to us.

"All authority in heaven and on earth" today belongs to Christ. To pray powerfully and to use spiritual authority effectively we have to be in sync with Christ himself. If we think like he thinks and want what he wants then he can trust us to use his delegated authority in the way he wants it used. And he will!

God has chosen to work on earth through the prayers and by the authority he has given to his people. What is it that he wants to do through you?

Something to **Think** About

◆ What is happening in your life that is clearly from the evil one? How can you pray or what can you do to curtail his activities?

◆ How can you pray or what can you do to enforce Christ's rule in your community?

Something to **Pray** About

◆ *Praise* Jesus who has "all power and authority in heaven and on earth."

◆ *Thank* God that he has made it possible for you to curtail the evil activities of Satan by prayer.

◆ *Ask* God to help you know when and where and how to use the spiritual authority he has given you.

◆ *Intercede* for the spiritual freedom of those held in Satan's grip.

Something to **Act** On

Identify one way that evil is operative in your personal world. Ask God to make clear what he wants to happen. Pray and do what you can to make that happen.

Prayer and Divine Healing

Is anyone among you in trouble? Let them pray. Is anyone happy? Let them sing songs of praise. Is anyone among you sick? Let them call the elders of the church to pray over them and anoint them with oil in the name of the Lord. And the prayer offered in faith will make them well; the Lord will raise them up. If they have sinned, they will be forgiven. Therefore confess your sins to each other and pray for each other so that you may be healed. The prayer of a righteous person is powerful and effective.
JAMES 5:13-16, (TNIV)

God is a healer. Healing is one of his specialties. Not only did he create our world, our bodies, our minds and our spirits, but he also cares for them. Though God made the world perfect and free from all disease, sin came in through Adam's disobedience so that now humans, along with the created order, are subject to frustration and the "bondage of decay" (Rom. 8:20-21).

God is in the business of healing what has been ruptured by sin. We see his healing hand already in Old Testament times. He is known as the God who heals. He promised the nomadic Hebrews on their way to the promised land, "I will not bring on you any of the diseases I brought on the Egyptians" (Ex. 15:26). David praises the Lord as one who "forgives all [my] sins and heals all [my] diseases" (Ps. 103:3).

Jesus' ministry was full of healings. Matthew tells us that "Jesus went throughout Galilee, teaching . . . preaching the good news of the kingdom, and healing every disease and sickness among the people" (4:23). Luke summarizes Jesus' ministry by telling us that "he went around doing good and healing all who were under the power of the devil, because God was with him" (Acts 10:38).

During the days of his ministry Jesus broadened the base of his healing powers by delegating healing powers to his disciples: "He called his twelve disciples to him and gave them authority . . . to heal every disease and sickness" (Matt. 10:1). Shortly before his departure Jesus transferred his healing powers to the whole church when he said, "Anyone who has faith in me will do what I have been doing" (John 14:12). That included healing, as his disciples were soon to discover.

James acknowledged the church's healing ministry when he urged sick persons to "call the elders of the church to pray over them and anoint them with oil in the name of the Lord." The church has always cared for and prayed for the sick. Elders are encouraged both to pray and to anoint with oil in the name of the Lord. Oil is a symbol in Scripture of the Holy Spirit. Anointing with oil reminds us that it is the Spirit's role to heal. Anointing and prayer go together. The anointing underscores God's role; prayer underscores the human role.

James comments further that "the prayer offered in faith will make them well; the Lord will raise them up." This is not a guarantee that every prayer will be answered exactly as we hope. It is, however, a confirmation that God's power for healing is released through prayer. In other words, we must ask with absolute confidence that God is able to heal and that prayer is his chosen way to do it. To heal is God's work; to ask is our work.

James concludes his remarks on healing prayer by adding, "The prayer of a righteous person is powerful and effective." With these words he confirms in yet another way that God's intent is to work through the prayers of his people. Something always happens when believers pray, that wouldn't have happened if they hadn't prayed. That's promise enough to send me to my knees. How about you?

Something to **Think** About
◆ Think of at least three different ways that people are healed. What is God's role in each of these?
◆ What difference does faith make when praying for healing? How can we increase the faith with which we pray?

Something to **Pray** About
◆ *Praise* God who is the healer of our diseases.
◆ *Thank* God for his role in healing all the diseases you have had in your lifetime.
◆ If you have doubted God's ability to heal or have questioned his goodness when he didn't heal in the way you wanted him to, *confess* that to the Lord.
◆ *Ask* God to heal any malady you now have whether large or small. Repeat this prayer regularly. God often heals gradually.
◆ *Intercede* for sick persons you know with the assurance that your prayers are powerful and effective.

Something to **Act** On
Next time you pray for healing try to imagine the positive result you are praying for. Mentally "seeing" the desired healing we are praying for is as much a prayer as our verbalizations.

WEEK SIX

✺

PRAYER AND FASTING

Prayer, Fasting, and God's Heart

*When you fast, do not look somber as the hypocrites do, for they dis-
figure their faces to show others they are fasting. Truly I tell you, they
have received their reward in full. But when you fast, put oil on your
head and wash your face, so that it will not be obvious to others that
you are fasting, but only to your Father, who is unseen, and your Father, who sees what is done in secret, will reward you.*
MATTHEW 6:16-18 (TNIV)

Fasting is a voluntary abstinence from food for the sake of a spiritual purpose. By denying ourselves something in the natural realm we foster
something in the spiritual realm.

Our lives tend to be dominated by the mundane realities of the natural.
Our thoughts and plans often circle around food, money, entertainment, and
creature comforts. Some of this is good and necessary. However, it can get
to the point where our occupation with earthly matters so controls us that it
pushes our relationship with God to the back burner. When that is the case it
is time to do something about it. One life-changing thing we can do is to fast.
Fasting can loosen the ties that bind us to the material world and strengthen
the ties that bind us to God.

Fasting has to do with self-denial but it is much more than that. The goal of
fasting has to do primarily with God. When we fast we are willing to endure
natural hunger in order to intensify spiritual hunger. It is a way of saying, "God
you are more important to me than food!" Jesus reminded his hearers that true
fasting would be "obvious . . . to your Father, who is unseen." Fasting is not worth
much if it doesn't get us closer to the heart of God and lift us up spiritually.

Fasting is really a type of prayer. We have defined prayer as a love relationship with God. Fasting improves this love relationship by riveting our attention on God so that we begin to seek him with all our hearts. It is an enhanced
form of prayer. In the words of Ron Dunn, "Fasting is the perfect environment
for prayer and seeking the Lord. With fasting we detach ourselves from the
earth, and with prayer we attach ourselves to heaven" (*Pray Something*, pp.
162-163). Our prayer lives will never be what God intended them to be without fasting.

By his life and teaching Jesus called attention to the value of prayer and fasting as an integral part of the Christian life. Jesus fasted for 40 days as part of the preparation for his life's work. He began his teaching on fasting in the sermon on the mount by saying, "When you fast. . . ." He apparently assumed that would be a normal part of New Testament Christianity.

Jesus' first words of instruction on fasting were negative. "When you fast," he said, "do not look somber as the hypocrites do, for they disfigure their faces to show men they are fasting." He was not teaching that others should never know we are fasting, but rather that we should fast with proper motives.

However, Jesus concludes his instruction on fasting in Matthew 6:18 with a positive reminder that "your Father, who sees what is done in secret, will reward you." The first reward of fasting is increased intimacy with the Father. The highest blessing is the blessing of God himself. Time spent in quiet conversation with the Father is the way to the deeper recesses of the Father's love. It's hard to imagine a greater reward than that. Creature comforts such as food, entertainment, self-pursuits and personal desires simply do not compare.

Something to **Think** About

◆ What are some ways that you could detach from earthly things in order to attach more to heavenly things?

◆ Do you agree that "our prayer lives will never be what God intended them to be without fasting"? Why or why not?

Something to **Pray** About

◆ *Praise* God who is everywhere present, who sees in secret, and who rewards openly.

◆ *Thank* God for giving you prayer and fasting as a way for you to get close to his heart.

◆ If mundane realities dominate your life and hinder your relationship with God, *confess* that to God and make plans to change.

◆ *Ask* God to give you such a hunger for him that you are willing to endure natural hunger in order to satisfy your spiritual hunger.

Something to **Act** On

Set a time to fast. Consider a food fast from after dinner one day to before dinner the next day. Plan to use the time you do not eat to seek the face of God.

Prayer, Fasting, and Divine Guidance

While they were worshiping the Lord and fasting, the Holy Spirit said, "Set apart for me Barnabas and Saul for the work to which I have called them." So after they had fasted and prayed, they placed their hands on them and sent them off.
ACTS 13:2-3

[I was] in weariness and toil, in sleeplessness often, in hunger and thirst, in fastings often, in cold and nakedness—besides the other things . . . my deep concern for all the churches.
2 CORINTHIANS 11:27-28 (NKJ)

Most of us are pretty deaf when it comes to "hearing" God's voice and getting his guidance. But there is a way to sharpen our spiritual hearing. New Testament Christians found that way. They fasted and prayed, and then they heard the Holy Spirit speak.

Praying for divine guidance was a common practice in the New Testament church. Luke reports, for example, that, "While they were worshiping the Lord and fasting, the Holy Spirit said, 'Set apart for me Barnabas and Saul for the work to which I have called them.'" Fasting and prayer not only helps us know the heart of God. It also helps us know the mind of God, in this case, his plan. God wanted the gospel to break out of its narrow boundaries and spread to the ends of the earth. His plan involved sending men to preach the word of God. He revealed his plan to believers as they worshiped and fasted. He even included the names of those who were to be the missionaries. This incident, though seemingly small, had a very large meaning for the expansion of Christianity. Prayed-up, fasted-up believers heard the Holy Spirit and implemented God's plan.

Some time later Paul and Barnabas's ministry success necessitated appointing elders in the newly planted churches. Once again it was with fasting and prayer that they discerned God's will and ordained his leaders of choice. Luke reports that they "appointed elders for them in each church and, with prayer and fasting, committed them to the Lord" (Acts 14:23).

Prayer and fasting was clearly a critical factor in Paul's life and ministry. In describing the trials of his ministry he includes the fact that he was "in fastings often." Ministry for Paul was not about finding a workable human strategy or "ten new ways to grow your church." Ministry was about fasting and praying in order to hear God's voice and discover his plan. Ministry was more important to Paul than food or drink.

Fasting works to open our ears and to make us receptive to the Holy Spirit's guidance. Imagine what life would be like if we acknowledge God in all our ways and he always directed our paths (Prov. 3:6). Imagine how many rash decisions and unwise choices would be avoided if the wisdom and understanding of the Holy Spirit were always in them.

I once heard a pastor report to his congregation that the ruling body of the church never made a decision without asking for God's guidance and being certain that it was the Lord's will. My first reaction was a mild, "Yes, that's a good way to go." However, before long I was saying to myself, "Wow! Imagine what a church could be if the Holy Spirit really directed every decision."

What worked for the Antioch church and what worked for Paul will work for any church or any believer today. We have with the same God. His ways have not changed. He is just as interested in guiding your life as he was in guiding early believers. So, if you have decisions to make, and if your spiritual ears need opening, why not get his guidance the way early Christians did—by prayer and fasting.

Something to **Think** About

- ◆ What might be the outcome if the leaders of your church fasted and prayed over every major decision?
- ◆ How might your life be different if you prayerfully sought God's will in every major decision, even if it sometimes meant you had to fast?

Something to **Pray** About

- ◆ *Praise* the all-wise Holy Spirit who is by our side at all times to guide us.
- ◆ *Thank* God for giving us prayer and fasting as a way to discern his will.
- ◆ If you are making decisions without seeking God's guidance, *confess* that to the Lord.
- ◆ *Ask* God to give you a spirit of dependence on him and his guidance.

Something to **Act** On

Seek God's will when you have a major decision to make and ask him to confirm his will in three different ways: through Scripture, circumstances, and an inner conviction from the Spirit.

Prayer, Fasting, and Divine Protection

Some men came and told Jehoshaphat, "A vast army is coming against you. . . ." Alarmed, Jehoshaphat resolved to inquire of the Lord, and he proclaimed a fast for all Judah. The people of Judah came together to seek help from the Lord.

2 CHRONICLES 20:2-4

(FOR THE WHOLE STORY READ 2 CHRONICLES 20:1-30)

I proclaimed a fast, so that we might humble ourselves before our God and ask him for a safe journey for us and our children, with all our possessions. . . . We fasted and petitioned our God about this, and he answered our prayer. EZRA 8:21, 23

We are living in the midst of a hostile environment. Paul says as much in Ephesians: "Our struggle is not against flesh and blood, but against the rulers, against the authorities, against the powers of this dark world and against the spiritual forces of evil in the heavenly realms" (6:12). Evil forces are invading our society today through pornography, media addiction, drug and alcohol addictions, gaming and gambling, sexual perversion, antimarriage and antifamily agendas, and a host of self-sins. Vulnerable to attacks of this nature, we need the protection that comes from God.

The Bible teaches us to think of prayer and fasting as key elements in divine protection. That was true, for example, in the story of Jehoshaphat king of Judah. Confronted by a vast multinational army with the potential power to crush Judah, Jehoshaphat "proclaimed a fast for all Judah." In response "the people of Judah came together to seek help from the Lord." Humbly in prayer they said, "We do not know what to do, but our eyes are upon you" (2 Chron. 20:12). As a result God heard their prayers, spoke words of reassurance, and then came to their defense thoroughly routing the enemy. The day of deliverance ended with a joyful celebration.

Ezra also thought he should appeal for God's protection by means of prayer and fasting. He was preparing to lead a large group of Jewish captives from

Persia back to Jerusalem. Though God had directed this mission, Ezra did not presume upon God and conclude that prayer was not needed. He understood that divine protection was not automatic. "I proclaimed a fast," said Ezra, "so that we might humble ourselves before our God and ask him for a safe journey for us and our children, with all our possessions." They prayed trusting that "the gracious hand of our God is on everyone who looks to him" (Ezra 8:22). God heard their prayers and acknowledged their fast. His answer was the gift of divine protection that they asked for and needed.

The lesson of prayer, fasting, and divine protection is an important one. God wants to protect us just as much as he wanted to protect the people we meet in the stories of Jehoshaphat and Ezra. But we do need to ask. With evil forces disrupting society, countering the truth of the gospel, and seeking to destroy the church there is need for prayer and fasting. Christians who are struggling with sins like lust, greed, addictions, anger, and selfish ambitions should be doing battle against these acts of the sinful nature with fasting and prayer. Parents and grandparents need to fast and pray for God to deliver their children and grandchildren from evil. We need multitudes of Christians seeking the Lord in fasting and prayer for the protection of his church and of our nations.

God promises to protect us from our enemies, but his protection does not come automatically. We have a responsibility in securing that protection. We have to ask. We may even have to enhance our asking by fasting. Is that something that you are ready for?

Something to **Think** About
◆ What does fasting add to prayer? When might God want you to add fasting to prayer?
◆ Why is prayer necessary to secure God's protection? Why doesn't God just always protect us automatically?

Something to **Pray** About
◆ *Praise* God for the power he has to provide the protection he promises.
◆ *Thank* God for the way he protected you physically and spiritually in the past.
◆ If, in looking back, you become aware that you have taken God for granted, *confess* that to him.
◆ *Ask* God to help you be alert to your need for his protection in the future and to ask him for it.
◆ *Intercede* for the physical, emotional, and spiritual protection of family members and friends.

Something to **Act** On
Tell God you are willing to accept a prayer and fasting assignment from him. Ask him for directions. Wait on his directions. Carry out the assignment that he gives.

Prayer, Fasting, and Spiritual Restoration

Declare a holy fast; call a sacred assembly. Summon the elders and all who live in the land to the house of the Lord your God, and cry out to the Lord....

"Even now," declares the Lord, "return to me with all your heart, with fasting and weeping and mourning. Rend your heart and not your garments. Return to the Lord your God, for he is gracious and compassionate, slow to anger and abounding in love, and he relents from sending calamity."
JOEL 1:14, 2:12-13

Something was wrong, seriously wrong, in the promised land. God's people had a problem, a sin problem so huge that God could not and would not ignore it. Ezekiel is explicit about the details. Sin, he said, was corrupting every layer of society. Priests were violating the law and failing to distinguish right from wrong. Political leaders were "on the take." Prophets were whitewashing the misdeeds of the politicians. Extortion was widespread. Robbery was pandemic. Poor people and foreigners were being mistreated. Justice had disappeared from the land (Ezek. 22:23-29).

God, who cannot and will not tolerate sin, decided to act—not to punish his people but to chastise them and bring them back to himself. He brought upon them a huge calamity—a massive locust plague together with drought. The devastation that followed touched everything: fields, grain, grapevines, olive trees, wheat and barley, fig trees, pomegranates, palm trees, and apple trees. They are all dried up, says Joel, and "the joy of mankind is withered away" (Joel 1:10-12).

Is there any hope, anything that will cause God to relent and restore his people? Joel's answer, really God's answer, is "yes"! "Declare a holy fast; call a sacred assembly. Summon the elders and all who live in the land to the house of the Lord your God, and cry out to the Lord, 'Return to me with all your heart, with fasting and weeping and mourning.'"

God always hears the cry of the repentant. God always responds to those

76

whose true repentance leads to fasting, weeping, and mourning.

What will happen if they fast and weep and mourn? "The Lord . . . will take pity on his people" (Joel 2:18). What will he do after they have repented? "I will repay you for the years the locusts have eaten. You will have plenty to eat until you are full" (2:25-26). What about the future? "Afterward, I will pour out my Spirit on all people . . . and everyone who calls on the name of the Lord will be saved" (2:28, 32).

What about sin problems that we face today? What should we do about personal lapses, family faults, church schisms, or national wrongdoing? How can we be restored if we have sinned and offended God? The answer today is still the same. There is only one way, God's way. "Return to me with all your heart, with fasting and weeping and mourning. Rend your heart and not your garments."

But will that really make a difference? Does God still respond in the same way? The answer is "Yes"! God is the same yesterday, today, and forever. He has not changed. "He is gracious and compassionate, slow to anger and abounding in love, and he relents from sending calamity."

Sin is just as offensive to God today as it ever was in the past. He will not tolerate sin today any more that he would in the past; but he will forgive it. Forgiveness and full restoration is offered to all who are truly repentant—to those who fast and weep and mourn over sin. He has made provision to forgive through Jesus Christ, by his atoning death on the cross. And "everyone who calls on the name of the Lord will be saved."

Something to **Think** About
   ◆ Why do you think God hates sin so much? Why can't he just ignore it?
   ◆ What is the difference, in God's dealing with us, between punishment and chastisement?

Something to **Pray** About
   ◆ *Praise* God for his wrath—his hatred of and intolerance of sin.
   ◆ *Thank* God that he graciously forgives repentant sinners and relents from sending calamity.
   ◆ *Confess* any sin that God, through his Spirit, makes you aware of.
   ◆ *Ask* God to restore what he may have taken from you in a time of chastisement.

Something to **Act** On
Study Ezekiel 22:23-31 and notice what caused God's wrath, how his "fiery anger" could have been avoided, and why it was not. Would history have been different if God had found an intercessor to "build up the wall and stand . . . in the gap on behalf of the land" (22:30)?

Prayer, Fasting, and Joy

The word of the Lord Almighty came to me: "Ask all the people of the land and the priests, 'When you fasted and mourned in the fifth and seventh months for the past seventy years, was it really for me that you fasted?'"

This is what the Lord Almighty says: "The fasts of the fourth, fifth, seventh and tenth months will become joyful and glad occasions and happy festivals for Judah. Therefore love truth and peace."
ZECHARIAH 7:4, 8:19

A devotional on fasting is probably not the place where you would expect to read something about joy. But here it is. God, speaking through the prophet Zechariah, says their fasts "will become joyful and glad occasions."

Jewish exiles who had returned to the land of Israel after 70 years in captivity came to the priests at the house of the Lord in Jerusalem asking, "Should I mourn and fast in the fifth month, as I have done for so many years?" God's answer comes in the form of a rebuking question: "Was it really for me that you fasted?" The question is a pointed reminder that their fasts were really for themselves, not for him. They were self-pitying, not God-glorifying, fasts. They fasted because of the calamities that their sin had brought upon them, not because of their sin.

When fasting arises out of true repentance and a readiness to reverse the direction of our sinful lives, God hears and forgives and turns our fasting into rejoicing. This is what happened to Judah and Israel after 70 years in exile. They turned and the Lord relented. The Lord Almighty said to them, "I will not deal with the remnant of this people as I did in the past. . . . So will I save you, and you will be a blessing. . . . I have determined to do good again to Jerusalem and Judah" (Zech. 8:11, 13, 15). Because they had found forgiveness and restoration he now promises that "the fasts of the fourth, fifth, seventh and tenth months will become joyful and glad occasions and happy festivals for Judah. Therefore love truth and peace."

Fasts should be joyful! When we stop thinking of ourselves and rivet our attention on God, that's joy. When we loosen our ties to earth by denying ourselves food and attach ourselves to heaven, that's joy! When the highest blessing we seek is God himself, that's joy.

When I was young I always tried hard to make the celebration of holy communion very sorrowful. That's what I thought it was supposed to be. I thought I had to be sorry that my sins caused Jesus' death. I was supposed to grieve for Jesus, because he was "despised and rejected by men, a man of sorrows, and familiar with suffering (Isa. 53:3). But I could never quit make myself feel the sorrow I thought I was supposed to feel. Years later I discovered joy at the Lord's table. Oh yes, there was grief, momentary grief, that my sin had caused his suffering and death. But my grief quickly turned into joy as I was reminded, through the broken body and shed blood of Jesus Christ, that my sins were forgiven. And my Savior—the "man of sorrows"—suffers no more. He is risen and exalted to the right hand of the Father. His sorrow turned to joy. So has mine.

I think I learned what God was trying to teach the believers of Zechariah's day. By God's grace the grief of repentance can turn into joy and gladness. He has turned my fasts into "joyful and glad occasions and happy festivals" and I, with them, truly do "love truth and peace." I hope your fasts have turned into joy too!

Something to **Think** About
◆ What's the main difference between a wrong fast and a right fast?
◆ How do mournful fasts get turned into "joyful and glad occasions"?
◆ How is it that sorrow for sin can be short-lived and the joy of forgiveness long-lived?

Something to **Pray** About
◆ *Praise* the Lord for his forgiving grace.
◆ *Thank* him for providing a way to turn fasting and mourning into joy and gladness.
◆ If your religious exercises have been more self-oriented than God-glorifying that is something you will want to repent of.
◆ *Ask* God to turn your sorrows to joy, your anxieties to peace, and your fears to hope.

Something to **Act** On
Next time you take holy communion move thoughtfully, intentionally from sorrow for sin to the joy of forgiveness.

Week Seven

PRAYING WITH OLD TESTAMENT SAINTS

Abraham: A Mighty Prevailing Pray-er

The Lord said, "The outcry against Sodom and Gomorrah is so great and their sin so grievous that I will go down and see if what they have done is as bad as the outcry that has reached me."

Abraham approached him and said: "Will you sweep away the righteous with the wicked? What if there are fifty righteous people in the city? Will you really sweep it away and not spare the place for the sake of the fifty righteous people in it? Far be it from you to do such a thing—to kill the righteous with the wicked. . . . Will not the Judge of all the earth do right?"

The Lord said, "If I find fifty righteous people in the city of Sodom, I will spare the whole place for their sake.

Then Abraham spoke up again: "Now that I have been so bold as to speak to the Lord, though I am nothing but dust and ashes, what if the number of the righteous is five less than fifty? Will you destroy the whole city because of five people? . . . What if only forty are found there? . . . What if only thirty? . . . What if only twenty? . . . What if only ten can be found there?"

He answered, "For the sake of ten, I will not destroy it."
GENESIS 18:20-32

Abraham was a mighty prevailing pray-er. He stood with the Lord one day on a mountain top overlooking the cities of Sodom and Gomorrah—wicked cities that deserved to be destroyed because of their grievous sin—and successfully convinced God to spare these wicked cities for the sake of the righteous in them. How many righteous? How about 50, 45, 40, 30, 20, and finally only 10. With each new plea God's response was, "I will not destroy it."

Truth be told, it was God who initiated that prayer-conversation. God was talking to himself—"Shall I hide from Abraham what I am about to do?—and then, convinced by his knowledge and plans (see vv.17-19), he broached the subject and waited for Abraham's response. In other words, God wanted

Abraham to plead with him and prevail in prayer.

There are some important principles to be learned from Abraham's prevailing prayer. First, though he was bold in prayer, he also humbly acknowledged, "I am nothing but dust and ashes." When we stand in God's presence and are conscious of him, we are emptied of any sense of self-importance. That's a good place to begin in prayer.

Second, Abraham's appeal was based on the character of God: "Will not the Judge of all the earth do right?" He wanted God's justice and honor to triumph. God is never put off when we ask for a course of action that we believe to be consistent with his nature.

Third, Abraham prayed the heart of God. He was not praying simply for Lot and his family. He was asking God to spare the whole city for the sake of the righteous. God's readiness to agree to Abraham's appeal tells us that God himself desired to show mercy to the people of Sodom. Abraham's prayer reflects the very heart of God. And God no doubt was pleased with Abraham's pleadings.

Fourth, Abraham prayed with persistence. Six times he appealed to God, talking him down from 50 to 10 righteous persons, as the number needed to spare the city. In each instance God agreed and led him on. God was pleased, not bothered, by his persistence in prayer.

Though Sodom was not spared, Abraham's prayer was actually answered. God did not sweep away the righteous with the wicked. He brought Lot and his family out to a place of safety. At the same time God's judgment on Sodom and Gomorrah had an upside. It warned the world of the terrible price of sin. That too reflects God's loving concern for his world.

Something to **Think** About

- ◆ What motivated Abraham to pray this mighty prevailing prayer? Is there a lesson in this for us?
- ◆ What do we learn from this episode about God's way of looking at prayer? What do we learn about prayer?

Something to **Pray** About

- ◆ *Praise* God for being a merciful and compassionate God.
- ◆ *Thank* God that he is willing to be prevailed upon through prayer.
- ◆ *Ask* God to place the concerns of his heart on your heart and on to your prayer agenda.
- ◆ *Intercede*, Abraham-style, for persons or groups of persons who deserve punishment.

Something to **Act** On

Find three things, mentioned in your daily newspaper, that are grievous to God. Pray that God will, in his mercy, defer judgment and bring the offenders to repentance.

Moses: His Prayer Changed God's Mind

But Moses sought the favor of the Lord his God. "O Lord," he said, "why should your anger burn against your people, whom you brought out of Egypt with great power and a mighty hand? Why should the Egyptians say, 'It was with evil intent that he brought them out, to kill them in the mountains and to wipe them off the face of the earth'? Turn from your fierce anger; relent and do not bring disaster on your people. Remember your servants Abraham, Isaac and Israel, to whom you swore by your own self: 'I will make your descendants as numerous as stars in the sky and I will give your descendants all this land I promised them, and it will be their inheritance forever.'" Then the Lord relented and did not bring on his people the disaster he had threatened.
EXODUS 32:11-14

God was angry. When Moses was up on Mount Sinai getting the ten commandments from God, the Israelites were at the bottom of the mountain casting an idol in the shape of a calf and worshipping it. God was furious! He had every right to be.

God said to Moses: "I have seen these people, . . . and they are a stiff-necked people. Now leave me alone so that my anger may burn against them and that I may destroy them. Then I will make you into a great nation" (32:9-10). Moses took the words of God, "leave me alone," not as prohibiting prayer but as encouraging intercession as the only way God's mind could be changed. He discovered ground for hope where it seemed like there was none. With this subtle form of encouragement Moses stepped into the gap and pleaded for God to change his mind.

First, he reminded God that these were his people and that he had delivered them from bondage in Egypt "with great power and a mighty hand." Having claimed them as his people and having gone to such lengths to save them, it would not make sense to destroy them, would it?

Then Moses warned God (imagine that) that destroying the nation of Israel could cause his reputation to be tarnished in Egypt and far beyond. The report of their deliverance had spread to "all the earth" as God had predicted (Ex. 9:16). All that would be lost, Moses intimated, if God now wiped them out. And God listened.

Finally, Moses reminded God that he had made a covenant—a solemn agreement—with Abraham, Isaac, and Israel to give them countless descendants and a homeland, and that he had sworn an oath to them. "You can't break an oath," Moses was saying. "A promise is a promise."

Then, the most amazing thing happened. God changed his mind! We read, "Then the Lord relented and did not bring on his people the disaster he had threatened."

Once again God is teaching us, not only about himself, but also about the role of intercession in his governance of the world. Mighty intercessors remember God and his works, remember his promises, and are concerned for his honor. Intercessors are moved by what they know of God and his mercy to pray with compassion for those who may well be deserving of punishment. Intercessors who pray in this way truly reflect the heart of God and of his interceding Son, Jesus Christ.

In Moses we catch a glimpse of the world's greatest intercessor, Jesus Christ. His death was an intercessory act that spared us from spiritual destruction. Today he lives to make intercession for all who have been redeemed from the bondage of sin. Through his ongoing intercessory activity God's covenant promises to his children are guaranteed and God's honor is upheld in all the earth. Praise God for all his intercessors, especially for the one who serves at his right hand.

Something to **Think** About
◆ What hope do we have for an answer from God when we are praying for those who deserve punishment?
◆ How do you react to the idea that God governs the world through the prayers of his people? If that be true, what should we do?

Something to **Pray** About
◆ *Praise* God for his compassion toward all who deserve punishment.
◆ *Thank* God for those who have in the past pleaded for him to be merciful to you.
◆ If you have had but little compassion for lost persons *confess* that to the Lord of mercies and ask his forgiveness.
◆ *Ask* God to increase your compassion for those who live under judgment.

Something to **Act** On
Plead God's mercy for children of the covenant who have grown up in the church but have fallen away from the faith. Remind God of what he will gain if they turn back to him.

Nehemiah: A Leader on His Knees

When I heard these things, I sat down and wept. For some days I mourned and fasted and prayed before the God of heaven. Then I said: "O Lord, God of heaven, the great and awesome God, who keeps his covenant of love with those who love him and obey his commands, let your ear be attentive and your eyes open to hear the prayer your servant is praying before you day and night for your servants, the people of Israel. I confess the sins we Israelites, including myself and my father's house, have committed against you. . . . Remember the instruction you gave your servant Moses, saying, 'If you are unfaithful, I will scatter you among the nations, but if you return to me and obey my commands, then even if your exiled people are at the farthest horizon, I will gather them from there and bring them to the place I have chosen as a dwelling for my Name.' . . . O Lord, let your ear be attentive. . . . Give your servant success today by granting him favor in the presence of this man." NEHEMIAH 1:4-6, 8-9, 11

I once heard a pastor say, "I do the preaching. I leave the praying up to my people." That pastor had it wrong! Nehemiah had it right! He was a leader on his knees. Prayer shaped his life and undergirded his leadership role in rebuilding the walls of Jerusalem and laying new foundations for God's covenant community.

Nehemiah was a high-level official in the court of Artaxerxes, king of the Medo-Persian empire. When a Jewish brother reported to him the disgraceful condition of the Jewish remnant and the city of Jerusalem Nehemiah was devastated. He immediately began to fast and pray over the situation. How many strong leaders start by weeping over evil? The prayer that follows is a model worth emulating.

Nehemiah begins with adoration: "O Lord, God of heaven, the great and awesome God, who keeps his covenant of love." Praise to God always puts things in perspective and fortifies faith.

He then moves to heart-searching confession: "I confess the sins we Israelites, including myself and my father's house, have committed against you." Notice that he includes himself. He acknowledges his part in the problem. Good prayer never overlooks personal guilt.

Next, he pleads the promise God made to gather his people from the ends of the earth and bring them back to Jerusalem if they return to him and obey his commands. "It's time now," Nehemiah is saying to God. We have met your criterion. Now we humbly claim your promise and expect you to intervene in our behalf.

Finally, Nehemiah makes a forthright request to God, a request that will initiate the undertaking that will lead to the restoration of Jerusalem. His prayer is: "Give your servant success today by granting him favor in the presence of this man." "This man" was Artaxerxes for whom Nehemiah was cup-bearer. The "favor" he needed was to be released from his position and sent, with provisions, to rebuild the walls of Jerusalem.

Nehemiah didn't just pray about the problem. He was ready to be involved. He reported for duty. Prayer can easily be a cop-out: "God, here's a problem. Please do something about it, would you?" If, having prayed a prayer like that, you were to tune your ear to God, you might hear him saying something like, "I *am* concerned, but I normally work through people. Are you willing to do whatever I call you to do?" Nehemiah was. That's what made him a great leader.

Whether the difficult situations we face are large or small, here's a good pattern to follow. Start with praise; move on to confession; plead the promises of God; make a specific request; and then report for duty. God likes that kind of praying.

Something to **Think** About

- ◆ What could you learn, from Nehemiah's experience, about prayer? About being available?
- ◆ How grieved are you over "brokenness" in the church? Enough to fast? To pray? To mourn? To do something about it?

Something to **Pray** About

- ◆ *Praise* God as a promise-making, promise-keeping God.
- ◆ *Thank* God for his willingness to hear prayer, to forgive and to restore.
- ◆ *Ask* God to show you any disgraceful condition in your church or community that you should pray about and do something about.
- ◆ *Commit* to carry out any assignment that God gives you, no matter what the cost may be.

Something to **Act** On

Review the five steps in Nehemiah's prayer. Pick an issue that needs to be addressed and pray about it using the five steps.

Solomon: A Wise Man's Prayer

The Lord appeared to Solomon during the night in a dream, and God said, "Ask for whatever you want me to give you."

Solomon answered, "... Now, O Lord my God, you have made your servant king in place of my father David. But I am only a little child and do not know how to carry out my duties. ... So give your servant a discerning heart to govern your people and to distinguish between right and wrong."

The Lord was pleased that Solomon had asked for this. So God said to him. "Since you have asked for this and not for long life or wealth for yourself ... I will do what you have asked. I will give you a wise and understanding heart, so that there will never have been anyone like you, nor will there ever be. Moreover, I will give you what you have not asked for—both riches and honor."

1 KINGS 3:5, 7, 9-13

O ur prayers often reveal the kind of persons we are. Solomon had the humility to ask God for a discerning heart so that he could be effective for God. Our prayers also determine the kind of persons we become. Because he asked wisely and humbly God gave Solomon the wisdom to become the wisest man who ever lived.

It all began for Solomon when, at the start of his reign as king of Israel, he honored God with 1,000 burnt offerings. That night God came to Solomon in a dream with a straightforward offer, "Ask for whatever you want me to give you." With that promise God put into Solomon's hand the key that would unlock his future.

Instead of asking for something that would bring him personal glory—riches, honor, or long life—Solomon asked for the wisdom to be a good king and to see the difference between good from evil in any situation. God was so pleased with his wise request that he not only gave him what he asked—a wise and discerning heart—but also the riches and honor and long life that he had not asked for.

God knew that Solomon needed to be wise and discerning in order to rule Israel effectively. But he didn't just drop the wisdom on him. Instead he invited him to ask. God gives us the same opportunity that he gave to Solomon. "Ask," he says, "and it will be given to you. . . . Everyone who asks receives" (Matt. 7:7-8). "If any of you lacks wisdom, he should ask God, who gives generously to all . . . and it will be given to him" (James 1:5). When we ask and receive we are humbly acknowledging our need for God and our faith in his ability to supply.

In response to his prayer God supplied Solomon all that he needed to be successful in his life and ministry. That's always the way he treats those who serve him. The God who calls us into service always supplies what we need. Jesus promised the same to the disciples: "I chose you and appointed you to go and bear fruit—fruit that will last. Then the Father will give you whatever you ask in my name" (John 15:16). The God who gives children, gives believing parents the grace to bring them up in the fear and knowledge of the Lord. The God who gives us responsibilities, is committed to equipping us for those tasks. But he does want us to ask.

God is often gracious and generous beyond our requests, as he was with Solomon. Jesus emphasized that if we would "seek first his kingdom" then God would take care of the other things in life as well (Matt. 6:33).

Solomon's story and prayer reminds us that the person who seeks wisdom is already wise. Would that be you?

Something to **Think** About
- If God offered you whatever you wanted, what would you ask for?
- If God gave you whatever you wanted, who would benefit the most, God or you?

Something to **Pray** About
- *Praise* God for his wisdom and generosity.
- *Thank* God for his willingness to meet the real needs (not felt needs) of those who seek first the kingdom of God.
- If you have presumed that God was going to give you all kinds of things whether you asked for them or not, *confess* that you have taken him granted.
- *Ask* God for the wisdom that he promises to give (James 1:5).

Something to **Act** On
For additional insights on wisdom study 1 Corinthians 1:18-31 and 2:1-16. Note who it is that gives wisdom; why it is given; who has it and who doesn't; and the difference between godly wisdom and worldly wisdom.

Job: A Praying Father

In the land of Uz there lived a man whose name was Job. This man was blameless and upright; he feared God and shunned evil. He had seven sons and three daughters. . . . He was the greatest man among all the people of the East.

His sons used to take turns holding feasts in their homes, and they would invite their three sisters to eat and drink with them. When a period of feasting had run its course, Job would send and have them purified. Early in the morning he would sacrifice a burnt offering for each of them, thinking, "Perhaps my children have sinned and cursed God in their hearts." This was Job's regular custom.

JOB 1:1-5

Job was a righteous rich man. The phrase "righteous rich" sounds to our ears like an oxymoron—a phrase combining two contradictory terms. But Job was both. Wealth had not spoiled him. On top of that he was a great father and had a wonderful family that lived together in harmony. Wow! Put that all together and you have a person whom the Bible calls "the greatest man among all the people of the East."

Job paid close attention to his relationship with God and to his relationship with his sons and daughters. We are told that "he feared God and shunned evil" and also that he regularly sacrificed burnt offerings for each of his children. In Job's day sacrificial offerings were the way people spoke to God. In other words, the offerings were prayers on behalf of his sons and daughters.

Job understood something very important about parenting. He understood that God calls parents to be priests—persons who speak to God regularly in behalf of their children. Job was a true spiritual leader in his home. He bore his children on his heart and regularly lifted them up to God.

Several things about Job's remarkable prayer life impress us. First, we can't help but notice that his greatest concern is for the spiritual well-being of his sons and daughters. Not that they had done anything overtly wrong. But in the event that they had sinned in their hearts they needed to be purified. Job knew that sin was often more than an outward deed. What he spoke to God about with his burnt offerings was purity of heart. Only God could do something about the hearts of his children.

Second, Job's prayer-sacrifices were made in the presence of his sons and daughters. He sent for them so that the sacrifices he made for each one of them could be made in their presence and would speak directly to their hearts. Burnt offerings are made for sin. The slain lamb being consumed by fire on the altar spoke to his children of the serious nature of sin and taught them, like their father, to fear God and shun evil. The smoke rising into the heavens reminded them of the God above who hears and answers prayer.

Finally, Job interceded in this way for his sons and daughters with urgency and regularity. It was "early in the morning" that Job rose up to make these burnt offerings and, we are told, "this was Job's regular custom." What a father. What a faithful intercessor.

The religious education of our children cannot be left to the church, to Sunday school, or to a Bible club. We cannot turn over praying for our children or grandchildren to a pastor, an elder, or the church. This is a priestly responsibility that belongs first of all to parents. Take this lesson from a page of Job's life. If you have children or grandchildren, be a faithful intercessor and bring them into God's presence each day. Pray that the blood of Christ, who made the ultimate atoning sacrifice, may cover all their sin.

Something to **Think** About

- ◆ What does it mean to be a priest to your children or grandchildren? In what ways do they need to be "covered"?
- ◆ What are the benefits of praying for your children or grandchildren in their presence?

Something to **Pray** About

- ◆ *Praise* God as a gracious forgiving God who covers your sins by the blood of his Son.
- ◆ *Thank* God for godly parents, grandparents, or others who have prayed for you.
- ◆ If you have failed to be a faithful intercessor for those near you *confess* that failure to the Lord and seek his forgiveness.
- ◆ *Intercede* for the spiritual well-being of loved ones. Ask God to forgive their sins.

Something to **Act** On

Pray the prayer of Paul in Colossians 1:9-14 for your children or grandchildren. (For other prayers of Paul see Phil. 1:9-11; Eph. 1:15-19, 3:14-19.)

WEEK EIGHT

THE PRAYING CHURCH

They Devoted Themselves to Prayer

*They devoted themselves to the apostles' teaching and to the fellowship,
to the breaking of bread and to prayer.*
ACTS 2:42

But we will devote ourselves to prayer and to the ministry of the word
ACTS 6:4 (NASV)

The first Christians were truly devoted to prayer. The prayers at their prayer meetings were not short, shallow, bless-me kinds of prayers. Three times in the early chapters of Acts Luke uses the intense Greek word *proskartere*, often translated as "devoted to," to report on the strength of their commitment to prayer. The word literally means "to occupy oneself diligently with something" or "to persist in." It's the word used in Acts 1:14 to describe their first prayer meeting: "These . . . were all continually devoting themselves to prayer" (NASB). It's the word used in Acts 2:42 to characterize their community activities: "they devoted themselves . . . to prayer." It's the word used to explain the intent of their spiritual leaders to "devote [themselves] to prayer" (Acts 6:4, NASB). Do you get the picture? They were really committed to prayer.

Paul uses the same Greek word when he talks about prayer. For example, he instructs Colossian Christians: "Devote yourselves to prayer, being watchful and thankful" (Col. 4:2). He exhorts Roman Christians to be "devoted to prayer" (Rom. 12:12, NASB) and he urges Ephesian believers to pray devotedly for all the saints (Eph. 6:18). The New Testament writers could not have been clearer. Devotion to prayer was the norm for New Testament Christians.

Most of the above references to devoted prayer have to do with corporate prayer. Luke's list of activities to which the early Christians were devoted—teaching, fellowship, breaking of bread, and prayer—are all communal activities, including prayer. Acts 3 begins with a report of Peter and John on their way to a prayer meeting at the temple. In the next chapter believers have come together for prayer in response to the threat by Jewish leaders (4:23-31). Not long after that believers gathered in a home to pray for imprisoned Peter (Acts 12). That early Christians regularly gathered for group prayer is a biblical fact not to be denied.

Why, we may ask, were those first Christians so devoted to prayer? The answer is that this is what they saw in the life of Jesus. He spent entire nights in prayer. He bathed the key moments of his life in prayer. His words, his miracles, his power all came through prayer. He gave his disciples a pattern for prayer (Matt. 6:9-13) and taught them to pray with boldness and persistence (Luke 11:5-8, 18:1-8). The first Christians simply continued with what they saw in Jesus' life and heard from his lips.

Unfortunately most of today's Western church does not share this same devotion to prayer. Saying prayers now-and-then to try and get our problems solved is not devotion to prayer. Rehearsing me-oriented prayer lists before God is not devotion to prayer. Prayer groups that spend most of their time sharing and a few minutes in prayer can hardly be called devoted to prayer.

God's Word pictures a church that was devoted to prayer, that persisted in prayer, and that occupied itself diligently with prayer. That is what God expects. That is what Jesus taught. That is what the New Testament Church modeled.

If you are a child of God, a Word-oriented Christian, and a member of this same New Testament church, then Paul is speaking to you: "Devote yourselves to prayer, being watchful and thankful" (Col. 4:2).

Something to **Think** About
- Why do modern day churches seem to lack the kind of devotion to prayer that we see in the early Christians?
- What will it take to increase your devotion to personal prayer? Devotion to corporate prayer?

Something to **Pray** About
- *Praise* Jesus Christ, the Son of God, as the best pray-er this world has ever known.
- *Thank* God for the privilege of prayer and for the model of the New Testament Christians who prayed with such devotion.
- If you see sinful apathy toward prayer in the church today, *confess* that to the Lord.
- *Ask* God to make you a person of prayer and to increase your devotion to prayer.
- *Intercede* for your church's corporate prayer life. Pray that increasing numbers may become devoted to prayer.
- *Commit* to spending increased amounts of time in prayer.

Something to **Act** On
Read Acts 1:14, 2:42, 6:4; Romans 12:12; Ephesians 6:18, and Colossians 4:2 with an awareness that the Greek word for "devoted to" is used in each of these passages. Let the message of these verses sink in.

Everyone Got
to the Prayer Meeting

[Jesus] was taken up before their eyes. . . . Then they returned to Jerusalem from the hill called the Mount of Olives, a Sabbath day's walk from the city. When they arrived, they went upstairs to the room where they were staying. . . . They all joined together constantly in prayer, along with the women and Mary the mother of Jesus, and with his brothers.
ACTS 1:9, 12-14

The first thing the disciples did after Jesus ascended to heaven was to pray, not each privately in their own homes, but together in an upstairs room. Jesus had ascended to heaven from the Mount of Olives. Immediately after he left them the disciples made their way, a distance of about a half mile, to an upstairs room for prayer. Once there "they all joined together constantly in prayer."

Why were they so eager to get to a prayer meeting? The answer is, first of all, out of obedience. Seven times in the week preceding his death Jesus had urged them to *ask* in prayer; and with good reason. Their ability to do what he was doing would depend on their *asking* (John 14:12-14). Their fruitfulness in ministry would be linked to their *asking* (John 15:16). Even their joy was related to *asking* (John 16:24). So now, responding to Jesus' promptings, they come together to *ask*.

A second reason why they hurried to the upper room for prayer was that they needed the Holy Spirit. Without the Spirit they were helpless. Jesus, knowing that they couldn't get along without the Spirit, commanded them, "Do not leave Jerusalem but wait for the gift my Father promised" (Acts 1:4). The gift they waited for was the Holy Spirit.

Waiting clearly meant for them both waiting and praying—waiting for and praying for the Spirit who would take the place of Jesus (John 14:16), who would teach them all things (John 14:26), and who would clothe them with power from on high (Luke 24:49). This was the gift the Father had promised (Acts 1:4-5). So they waited and prayed for the coming of the One who would make all the difference.

Remarkably, everyone got to that first prayer meeting. Luke reports that "they all joined together constantly in prayer, along with the women and Mary the mother of Jesus, and with his brothers." This was the praying church at its best. Luke uses two key words to describe this prayer meeting. One is the Greek word for "devoted." They were devoted to prayer—focused, energized, passionate prayer. The second word is the Greek word for "with one mind." Those who prayed in that upper room were of one mind. They were together physically but more importantly they were together spiritually. They were spiritually one.

Ten days later, on the day of Pentecost, they were once again all together in one place praying when, with the sound of a violent wind and the appearance of flames of fire, their prayers were answered and they were "all filled with the Holy Spirit" (Acts 2:4).

Corporate prayer was a high priority for the first Christians. They prayed with each other. They prayed with devotion. They prayed with one heart and mind. Devotion to corporate prayer continued to be a priority for the early church. Of the 43 references to prayer in the book of Acts, 26 relate to corporate prayer.

The church planted by Jesus' disciples valued corporate prayer. Jesus had prepared them for this. It was his vision. It's still his vision today. Anything less is less than Jesus intended.

Something to **Think** About
◆ What does the corporate prayer model of the first Christians mean for us today? Should corporate prayer be a priority?
◆ Do you think the corporate prayers of the Jerusalem church fueled the explosive evangelism that was soon to follow?

Something to **Pray** About
◆ *Praise* God who hears and answers prayer.
◆ *Thank* him that the gift of the Holy Spirit was given for all believers, including us today.
◆ If your church is apathetic about corporate prayer you may want to offer a prayer of *repentance* for it as Daniel did for the erring nation of Israel (Dan. 9:4-19).
◆ *Intercede* for your church and ask God to bring it to the place where "all join together constantly in prayer."

Something to **Act** On
If your church doesn't provide an opportunity for you to pray with other Christians, ask God to send you one other person as a prayer partner. Build a prayer group beginning with the two of you.

The Blessing of "Agreeing Prayer"

I tell you that if two of you on earth agree about anything you ask for, it will be done for you by my Father in heaven. For where two or three come together in my name, there am I with them.
MATTHEW 18:19-20

These all with one mind were continually devoting themselves to prayer, along with the women, and Mary the mother of Jesus, and with His brothers. ACTS 1:14 (NASB)

To describe the "agreement" of believers praying together on earth Jesus used a familiar sounding word. In the Greek Bible it is *sumphoneo*, which means "sound together." In English it is usually translated symphony. Jesus used this word of Christians who, though as different as instruments in an orchestra, prayed together with one mind and one heart. Their prayers "sound together" in the ears of God.

Jesus places great value on believers praying in agreement. He says, "If two of you earth agree about anything you ask for, it will be done for you by my Father in heaven." The Father wants his children to come together in "agreeing" prayer so that his power will be released and his purposes accomplished on earth in response to their prayers.

What makes "agreeing" prayer work is not simply a group of believers coming together to pray, but rather believers who find Spirit-given, heartfelt harmony in prayer. Something happens when believers come together in concerted prayer that doesn't happen through individual prayer. One-accord prayers on earth bring heaven into line with what's happening here on earth.

The "agreeing" prayer that Jesus spoke of before he left soon became a reality in the church. In the very first prayer meeting believers were "all with one mind. . . continually devoting themselves to prayer" and when the spiritual leaders were told to stop speaking of Jesus we read "they all, with one mind, made prayer to God" (4:24 BBE). God responded to their "agreeing" prayers by filling them with the Holy Spirit and by shaking the building where they were meeting.

When believers pray together "with one mind" several wonderful things can be expected to happen. First, they are able to *discern the will of God*. Jesus taught that agreeing prayer is prayer in Jesus' name. To pray in Jesus' name is to pray in union with him and in harmony with his will and purposes. When each of two or more believers hears God speak through his Spirit and each discerns God's will, then when they come together in prayer, they can agree in prayer and pray "in accord with his will."

Second, their *prayers are answered*. God promises to answer "agreeing" prayer. What they have asked "will be done . . . by my Father in heaven," says Jesus. When "earth" discovers and asks in accord with "heaven's" will, then "heaven" will act in accord with "earth's" prayer.

Third, pray-ers *will experience Christ's presence*. Christ promises to be with believers who come together in his name. What they experience is Christ's manifest presence, something more than simply knowing that God in Christ is everywhere present. His manifest presence gives "agreeing" pray-ers assurance that he is there to bless them, to guide them, and to hear and answer their prayers.

Finally, believers who pray "agreeing" prayer *will experience the wonder of Christian community*. Unity in prayer fosters community. United in Christ, they are also united with each other. Experiencing the presence of Christ, they experience anew the presence of others in whom Christ dwells.

God promises to bless in these wonderful ways those who "agree" in prayer. But a promise only has value if it is claimed. God makes this promise to you. Do you have plans to claim it?

Something to **Think** About

- Which of the four blessings that flow from "agreeing" prayer have you experienced?
- What could a church do to encourage more "agreeing" prayer?

Something to **Pray** About

- *Praise* God as a promise-making, promise-keeping, prayer-answering God.
- *Thank* God for making his will known, for manifesting himself to you in unique ways, and for hearing and answering prayer.
- If "agreeing" prayer is missing entirely from your life and/or your church, *confess* that to the Lord.
- *Ask* God to give you opportunities for "agreeing" prayer.

Something to **Act** On

Choose one other believer and agree to pray together for the Spirit's fruit of love, joy and peace mentioned in Galatians 5:22. This would be a prayer in accord with God's will.

A God-Focused
Prayer Meeting

They raised their voices together in prayer to God. "Sovereign Lord,"
they said, "you made the heaven and the earth and the sea, and every-
thing in them. You spoke by the Holy Spirit through the mouth of your
servant, our father David:
    "'Why do the nations rage
    and the people plot in vain?
        The kings of the earth take their stand
    and the rulers gather together against the Lord
    and against his Anointed One.'"
                              ACTS 4:24-26

All prayer meetings should be God-focused. But it's not easy to keep them that way. If you have been in prayer meetings you know how quickly your mind can flit *to* the things you are praying for and *away from* the God you are praying to. There is much to be gained if we can keep our eyes fixed on him.

Years ago J. B. Phillips wrote a book entitled *Your God is Too Small.* He reminded us that the ways we imagine God often reduce him to small proportions quite unlike the God he really is. It's important when we pray that our God be VERY BIG. Trusting him to hear and answer prayer depends on our knowing just how great he really is.

The early Christians, who we read about in Acts 4, had a "big" God. After being told by Jewish authorities never again to teach in the name of Jesus, they "raised their voices together in prayer to God." "Sovereign Lord," they said, "you made the heaven and the earth and the sea, and everything in them. . . ." Their God was big enough to have created the world. If you know that God is that "big" you don't need to be anxious about the threats of puny human leaders. The early Christian pray-ers were not afraid!

And, since God had created the world, he could surely manipulate the created order and do miracles. So they prayed, "Stretch out your hand to heal and perform miraculous signs and wonders" (Acts 4:30). And God did! (See Acts 5:12-16.)

God also had a plan for history and the foreknowledge of what lay ahead. They found in Psalm 2 that portion of God's plan that applied to them in their current situation. They quoted the words of that psalm back to God and reminded him that his power and will had decided these things beforehand (Acts 4:28). People who remember that God has a plan and knows the future can pray with boldness and confidence.

Good prayer meetings usually begin with praise. Praise *focuses our hearts on God*. It raises the level of our God-consciousness and helps us see God for who he really is. When we come to God our needs and problems may seem overwhelming, but if we're conscious of God, we'll know that he is bigger than our problems and able to meet our needs. The level of our prayers will usually equal the level of our praise.

God-focused prayer will also *strengthen our faith*. Focus on God and your thoughts will be occupied with his power, his wisdom, his love and his faithfulness. You will recall what he has done and will be confident of what he can do. Such thoughts have the ability to increase our faith. People who focus on God find their faith growing strong.

Finally, God-focused prayer *gives courage*. Courage flows from what we know about God and his purposes. If we know that God has already defeated Satan and that he "will soon crush Satan under [our] feet" (Rom. 16:20); and if we know that "the weapons we fight with . . . have divine power to demolish strongholds" (2 Cor. 10:4), then we will pray with courage. God-focused prayer gives us the spirit of triumph.

God-focused prayer is powerful, effective, faith-filled prayer. That's how early Christians prayed. And that's the way God wants you and me to pray too.

Something to **Think** About

◆ How "God-focused" are your personal prayer times? Your church's prayer meetings?

◆ How could the God-focus be increased in your prayer times? In your church's prayer meetings?

Something to **Pray** About

◆ *Praise* God who made the heavens and the earth and the sea, and everything in them.

◆ *Thank* God for the courage, strength, and peace he gives you when you focus your eyes on him.

◆ If your prayers have lacked a God-focus *confess* that to the Lord.

◆ *Ask* God to give you a greater consciousness of him every time you pray.

Something to **Act** On

Start your intentional prayer times by meditation on one or more of God's attributes. Try to link that attribute to your own personal world.

God's Earth-Shaking Answer

After they prayed, the place where they were meeting was shaken. And they were all filled with the Holy Spirit and spoke the word of God boldly. . . . With great power the apostles continued to testify to the resurrection of the Lord Jesus, and much grace was upon them all.
ACTS 4:31, 33

God loves to answer prayer. Not just any and every prayer, of course, but particularly prayers that are in accord with his will. God doesn't answer prayers that are wrongly motivated (James 4:3), that lack faith (James 1:6), or that come from a sinful heart (Ps. 66:18). But when believers pray in faith, with one mind, in Jesus' name, in accord with God's will, and ask for strength to serve him—that's a different matter. Then God takes pleasure in the prayers of his people and is eager to answer them. That was clearly the case with the prayers of the first beleaguered Christians of whom we read in Acts 4.

The first evidence that God was pleased with their prayers came in a very tangible form. After they had prayed "the place where they were meeting was shaken." This was apparently God's way of saying: "I am with you! I have heard your prayers! You can count on me!"

Following the shaking we read that "they were all filled with the Holy Spirit." In other words they came under the influence of the Spirit of God to the point where they experienced the presence of Christ, were strengthened in faith, and were given a holy boldness to "obey God rather than men" (Acts 5:29).

What followed were even more specific answers to prayer. They asked God to "enable your servants to speak your word with great boldness" (Acts 4:29). Luke reports the answer, they "spoke the Word of God boldly." However, God's answer to their prayer was not just a one-shot response. After that initial burst of Spirit-filled boldness the apostles "continued to testify to the resurrection of the Lord Jesus."

The need for witness to the gospel continued. Not long after that the apostles found themselves back in prison. God sent an angel who came during the night and opened the doors of the jail. The angel said to them, "Go, stand in the temple courts . . . and tell the people the full message of this new life." They obeyed. They entered the temple courts at daybreak and "began to teach the people" (Acts 5:20-21). Through this experience God was answering their prayer for boldness to speak the word.

They also asked God to continue to "heal and perform miraculous signs and wonders through the name of Jesus" (Acts 4:30). God had an answer for that prayer too. The apostles were so endued with power from the risen Lord that they performed "many miraculous signs and wonders among the people" to the point where "people brought the sick . . . and crowds gathered also from the towns around Jerusalem, bringing their sick and those tormented by evil spirits, and all of them were healed" (Acts 5:12, 15-16). Talk about earth-shaking answers to prayer!

Finally, we read that "much grace was upon them all." God's grand and overarching answer to their prayers was the gift of much grace—grace to be witnesses, grace for boldness, grace for endurance, grace even for disgrace. After being flogged by authorities for speaking in the name of Jesus the apostles "left the Sanhedrin, *rejoicing* because they had been counted worthy of suffering disgrace for the Name" (Acts 5:41).

The golden-mouthed Chrysostom once said, "God can refuse nothing to a praying congregation." It certainly appears that he refused nothing to that first praying church of Jerusalem. What do you suppose would happen if a congregation prayed that way today?

Something to **Think** About
- ◆ What would cause God to take pleasure in your prayers and be eager to answer them?
- ◆ What kind of prayer could you pray that might prompt God to answer by filling you with his Holy Spirit?

Something to **Pray** About
- ◆ *Praise* the Lord as a gracious and giving God.
- ◆ *Thank* him for hearing and answering the prayers of believers in powerful and amazing ways.
- ◆ *Confess* before God any sin patterns in your life that hinder prayer.
- ◆ *Ask* God to continue to grow your prayer life.

Something to **Act** On
Take some time in the next few days to review the prayer activities suggested in this devotional. Recall those that were most helpful. Continue to work on them.

THE JOY OF PRAYER

GUIDE FOR
GROUP STUDY

Introduction

The eight sessions in this companion study guide are thematically related to the eight weekly segments in *The Joy of Prayer* devotional.

Each study guide session begins with a "DVD Introduction" by the author, Alvin VanderGriend. Watch the DVD first. Then move to the "Group Interaction" questions which gives you opportunity to "React" to the presentation, "Share" from your own experience, and "Discuss" a related prayer issue. Next dig for truths on prayer in Scripture as you use discovery questions in the "Bible Study" segment. End your group session with the suggested "Closing Prayer Time."

After each group session, review the "Personal Prayer This Week" to reinforce what you learned. Read the five *Joy of Prayer* devotionals identified under the heading "Suggested Reading This Week," as these correspond with the session you just completed. Note that the devotionals can be used personally or in a family setting.

You are embarking on a journey that will invigorate your prayer life and help you enjoy God. God invites you to enjoy him and the sweetness of his love. He wants a love relationship with you. Prayer is at the heart of this relationship. I urge you, press on in your journey of learning to enjoy God through prayer. No effort in life will yield a greater blessing.

Note to Group Leaders

In the "Leader Notes" at the end of this book, find preparation helps as well as ideas on leading the group study.

✦

WEEK ONE

The Joy of Prayer

In this session we will learn that
- ◆ prayer is a pathway to joy.
- ◆ joy is found in every element of prayer.
- ◆ Jesus Christ is the "way" to joyful prayer.

DVD INTRODUCTION   (16 MINUTES)

Prayer is a pathway to joy

- ◆ Prayer leads to joy because it _____ _____ _____.

  You will fill me with joy in your presence, with eternal pleasures at your right hand. —PSALM 16:11

  ". . . these I will bring to my holy mountain and give them joy in my house of prayer." —ISAIAH 56:7

- ◆ The joy of prayer is the joy of _____ with God.

  Rejoice always; pray without ceasing; in everything give thanks. (NASB)
  —1 THESSALONIANS 5:16-18

Joy is found in every element of prayer

PRAISE

- ◆ The joy of praise is joy in God the _____.

  Shout for joy to the LORD, all the earth. Worship the LORD with gladness; come before him with joyful songs. Know that the LORD is God.
  —PSALM 100:1-3

- ◆ Our main purpose in life is "to glorify God and enjoy him forever."
  —WESTMINSTER SHORTER CATECHISM

THANKSGIVING

◆ The joy of thanksgiving is joy in the _____ of God the giver.

We pray . . . that you may live a life worthy of the Lord and may please him in every way: . . . joyfully giving thanks to the Father. —COLOSSIANS 1:10-12

CONFESSION

◆ The joy of confession is the joy of a _____ relationship with God.

O God, . . . blot out my transgressions. Wash away all my iniquity and cleanse me from my sin. Let me hear joy and gladness; . . . Restore to me the joy of your salvation and grant me a willing spirit, to sustain me.

—PSALM 51:1-2, 8, 12

ASKING

◆ The joy of asking is the joy of receiving what we have asked for

"_____ _____ _____."

"I tell you the truth, my Father will give you whatever you ask in my name. Until now you have not asked for anything in my name. Ask and you will receive, and your joy will be complete." —JOHN 16:23-24

Jesus Christ is the "way" to joyful prayer

◆ Jesus Christ is the great _____-_____.

◆ Christ opens the way to the Father's heart and the Father's throne.

GROUP INTERACTION   (10-15 MINUTES)

React

Would you expect a non-Christian to find joy in prayer? Why or why not?

Share

When has prayer been a joyful experience for you? Has it ever seemed a drag?

Discuss

If a Christian finds no joy in prayer what might be the problem? What helpful counsel might you give to a joyless pray-er?

BIBLE STUDY (10-15 MINUTES)

"I tell you the truth, my Father will give you whatever you ask in my name. Until now you have not asked for anything in my name. Ask and you will receive, and your joy will be complete." —JOHN 16:23, 24

---

1. Does "whatever" mean that we can ask for anything we want and expect to receive it?

2. To ask "in Jesus' name" means to ask for that which Christ desires. Give an example of a prayer that you know is "in Jesus' name." Give an example of a prayer that is not "in Jesus' name."

3. How did people ask before they asked "in Jesus' name"?

4. How could Jesus make such an absolute promise? Will it *always* hold true?

5. Describe the type of prayer that results in "complete joy."

CLOSING PRAYER TIME (10 MINUTES IN SMALL GROUPS)

Identify a number of things you know Jesus wants for you that you also want for yourselves. These are things you can ask for "in Jesus' name." For example, in James 1:5 God promises wisdom to believers who ask for it. So, to ask for wisdom is to pray "in Jesus' name." Take your list of "in-Jesus'-name" prayers into a small group prayer time. Ask these things for yourselves and for each other.

PERSONAL PRAYER THIS WEEK

Go for joy in your prayer times this week. Find joy in each element of prayer. Let *praise* give rise to joy as God becomes real to you. Let your *thanksgiving* make you conscious of what God has done in your life. Let *confession* restore the joy of a healed relationship. Let your *asking* "in Jesus' name" give you the complete joy of receiving what you asked for.

SUGGESTED READING THIS WEEK

Read the five *Week One* devotions in *The Joy of Prayer* (pp. 9-19).

✵

WEEK TWO

Praying With the Trinity

In this session we will learn that
- ◆ we pray *to* the Father.
- ◆ we pray *through* the Son.
- ◆ we pray *by* the Holy Spirit.
- ◆ the Father is eager to give the Holy Spirit to those who ask.

DVD INTRODUCTION   (18 MINUTES)
We pray *to* the Father

◆ Jesus taught us to address God as_____.

"This, then, is how you should pray: 'Our Father in heaven . . .'"
—MATTHEW 6:9

◆ Prayer is the communication of a loving, _____ - _____
relationship.

How great is the love the Father has lavished on us, that we should be called children of God! And that is what we are! —1 JOHN 3:1

◆ Knowing God as Father is essential to a _____ prayer life.

We pray *through* the Son

◆ Jesus _____ to make prayer possible.

◆ Jesus _____ to guarantee our access to the Father.

. . . he (Jesus) always lives to intercede for them (those who come to God through him). —HEBREWS 7:25

We pray *by* the Holy Spirit

Pray in the Spirit on all occasions with all kinds of prayers and requests.
—Ephesians 6:18

◆ To pray "in the Spirit" is to be _____ in prayer by the Spirit.

◆ The Holy Spirit is our _____ prayer assistant.
In the same way, the Spirit helps us in our weakness. We do not know what we ought to pray for, but the Spirit himself intercedes for us with groans that words cannot express. —Romans 8:26

◆ The Spirit enables us to pray like_____.

The Father is eager to give the Holy Spirit to those who ask

◆ Jesus _____ us to ask the Father for the Holy Spirit.
". . . how much more will your Father in heaven give the Holy Spirit to those who ask him!" —Luke 11:13

◆ The Father is _____ to give us the Holy Spirit.

GROUP INTERACTION   (10-15 MINUTES)

React

Should we try to be conscious of the three persons of the Trinity and their roles when we pray? What difference would it make?

Share

Share with others in your group how you usually address God when you pray. Is that form of address meaningful for you, or is it just a habit?

Discuss

There is no example in the Bible of believers praying to the Holy Spirit. Yet, when we sing Spirit songs like, *Spirit of the Living God*, we are really praying to the Spirit. Is it okay to pray to the Holy Spirit? Why or why not?

BIBLE STUDY (10-15 MINUTES)

"Which of you fathers, if your son asks for a fish, will give him a snake instead? Or if he asks for an egg, will give him a scorpion? If you then, though you are evil, know how to give good gifts to your children, how much more will your Father in heaven give the Holy Spirit to those who ask him!" —LUKE 11:11-13

1. What is the role of Jesus in this teaching? The role of the Father? The role of the Spirit? The role of prayer?

2. Name several good gifts Christian parents give to their children. Why do parents give these gifts? What do parents want most for their children?

3. Name several good gifts the Father gives his children. Why does he give these gifts? What's so special about the gift of the Holy Spirit?

4. How eager do you think the Father is for us to have the gift of the Holy Spirit? Why might he be eager?

5. Can anyone ask the Father for the gift of the Holy Spirit and receive him? How about disobedient Christians? How about non-Christians?

CLOSING PRAYER TIME   (10 MINUTES IN SMALL GROUPS)

Pray in your small group about the "gift" of the Holy Spirit. Try to use all of the elements of prayer as you pray. For example:

♦ *Praise* the Father as the gracious giver of the Holy Spirit.
♦ *Thank* the Father for his willingness to give you the Holy Spirit.
♦ *Confess* if you have not asked for the Spirit or have taken him for granted.
♦ *Ask* the Father to give you the Holy Spirit with all the blessings that he brings.
♦ *Promise* the Father that you are willing to be led by the Spirit.

PERSONAL PRAYER THIS WEEK

The word "ask" in the original Greek of this passage is literally "ask continually." In other words, Jesus is telling us to continually ask the Father for the Holy Spirit. So, ask the Father for the Holy Spirit *every day* in the coming week. Watch for the evidences of the Spirit in your life. Memorize Luke 11:13 so that it will always be there to remind you of the promise Jesus made.

SUGGESTED READING THIS WEEK

Read the five *Week Two* devotions in *The Joy of Prayer* (pp. 21-31).

❁

WEEK THREE

Hearing God in Prayer

In this session we will learn that
- ◆ God is a talker.
- ◆ believers are able to hear God speak.
- ◆ believers who listen to God are richly blessed.
- ◆ believers need to distinguish God's voice from other voices.
- ◆ to improve our "hearing" we have to improve our relationship.

DVD INTRODUCTION   (22 MINUTES)
God is a talker

◆ The _____ is God's primary way of speaking to us.

All Scripture is God-breathed and is useful for teaching, rebuking, correcting and training in righteousness, so that all God's people may be thoroughly equipped for every good work. —2 TIMOTHY 3:16-17 (TNIV)

◆ God can and does communicate with us directly by his_____.

But you received the Spirit of sonship. And by him we cry, "Abba Father." The Spirit himself testifies with our spirit that we are God's children.
                                                    — ROMANS 8:15-16

◆ God communicates with us in order to have a _____ love relationship with us.

Believers are able to hear God speak

◆ Jesus speaks to us in _____ that we can "hear."

"The sheep listen to his (the Shepherd's) voice . . . his sheep follow him because they know his voice." —JOHN 10:3-4

◆ Jesus _____ listening to the Father.

"I judge only as I hear." —John 5:30

"My teaching . . . comes from him who sent me." —John 7:16

"I . . . speak just what the Father has taught me." —John 8:28

"Whatever I say is just what the Father has told me to say." —John 12:50

Believers who listen to God are richly blessed

◆ By listening we receive _____ for daily living.

Trust in the Lord with all your heart and lean not on your own understanding; in all your ways acknowledge him, and he will make your paths straight. —Proverbs 3:5-6

◆ By listening we come to _____ God and Jesus.

"It is written in the Prophets: 'They will be taught by God.' Everyone who listens to the Father and learns from him comes to me." —John 6:45

Believers need to distinguish God's voice from other voices

◆ There are four possible voices that we can "hear": the _____, the _____, the _____, or the _____.

◆ Ask God to _____ _____ the "other" voices.

◆ Test what you "hear" by the nature and Word of God.

◆ If doubt remains ask God to _____ his communiqué.

To improve our "hearing" we have to improve our relationship

◆ _____ your mind toward God.

◆ _____ God for a listening ear.

◆ _____ yourself to hear.

◆ _____ God to speak.

◆ Be ready to_____.

GROUP INTERACTION (10-15 MINUTES)

React

How do you react to the idea that God is a talker? Do you think God is insulted if we don't listen to him?

Share

Share with your group a time when you were sure that you "heard" the Spirit.

Discuss

Would it be safer in trying to "hear" God, if we just stuck to the Bible and didn't fuss with "hearing" the Spirit? What might be lost if we took that approach?

BIBLE STUDY (10-15 MINUTES)

"The man who enters by the gate is the shepherd of his sheep. The watchman opens the gate for him, and the sheep listen to his voice. He calls his own sheep by name and leads them out. When he has brought out all his own, he goes on ahead of them, and his sheep follow him because they know his voice. But they will never follow a stranger; in fact, they will run away from him because they do not recognize a stranger's voice." —JOHN 10:2-5

"My sheep listen to my voice; I know them, and they follow me." —JOHN 10:27

---

1. Describe the shepherd/sheep relationship. What's to be gained if sheep listen to and follow their shepherd? What are the consequences if they don't?

2. In the John 10 analogy Jesus is the Shepherd and believers are sheep. What is the role of Jesus? What is true of believers?

3. What is implied in Jesus' observation that the Shepherd "calls his own sheep by name"?

4. What other voices are trying to get your attention? Why do they want you to hear their voices? What's the best way to respond to these "stranger" voices?

5. How does a Shepherd/believer relationship start? How does it develop?

CLOSING PRAYER TIME   (10 MINUTES IN SMALL GROUPS)

◆ Take some time in silence to prepare for prayer (2-3 minutes). Ask the Spirit to teach you how to talk to the Shepherd. Let the Spirit bring prayer thoughts to your mind. Does he want you to express *praise* or *thanks* to the Shepherd? Is there something he wants you to *confess*? Does he want you to *ask* for something? Does he want you to *commit* to follow the Shepherd?

◆ Verbalize out loud in your small group the thoughts the Spirit has brought to mind.

PERSONAL PRAYER THIS WEEK

Spend some time quietly listening for the Spirit's voice at the beginning of your prayer time each day. Invite him to bring thoughts to your mind from his Word or directly through his Spirit. Make sure that what you "hear" from the Spirit is not outside the boundaries of biblical truth. Pray about the things he has brought to mind.

SUGGESTED READING THIS WEEK

Read the five *Week Three* devotions in *The Joy of Prayer* (pp. 33-43)

✺

WEEK FOUR

Praying Jesus Way

In this session we will learn that
- ◆ we can pray like Jesus.
- ◆ Jesus grants requests that bring glory to the Father.
- ◆ prayer opens the floodgate of spiritual blessings.

DVD INTRODUCTION (16 MINUTES)
We can pray like Jesus

- ◆ Jesus _____ us into his relationship with the Father.

- ◆ We can _____ the Father as confidently as Jesus did.

- ◆ Believers who pray to the Father pray as members of his_____.

Jesus grants requests that bring glory to the Father

"I will do whatever you ask in my name, so that the Son may bring glory to the Father. You may ask me for anything in my name, and I will do it."
—JOHN 14:13-14

- ◆ The Father's glory was the prime_____ of Jesus life or earth.

- ◆ The Father's glory is the _____ factor in Jesus response to our prayers.

- ◆ Every _____of prayer is intended to glorify God.

Prayer opens the floodgates of spiritual blessings

"Ask and it will be given you; seek and you will find; knock and the door will be opened to you. For everyone who asks receives; he who seeks finds; and to him who knocks, the door will be opened. . . . how much more will your Father in heaven give good gifts to those who ask him!" —MATTHEW 7:7-8, 11

- ◆ Jesus is inviting us to ask for_____.

- ◆ Jesus wants us to have _____ _____ _____ for life and godliness.

- ◆ He _____ us to ask for spiritual blessings.

- ◆ He expects us to be _____ in our asking.

GROUP INTERACTION   (10-15 MINUTES)

React

What are some things Jesus thinks about in deciding whether or not to give us what we ask? What kind of requests can we make of Jesus that will bring glory to the Father?

Share

Can you remember what it was like to be a child? Share with your group what it feels like for *you* to be a *child* of your Father in heaven?

Discuss

Should we pray because we are commanded to do so, even if we don't feel like it; or should we pray only when we feel like it?

BIBLE STUDY   (10-15 MINUTES)

> *"Ask and it will be given you; seek and you will find; knock and the door will be opened to you. For everyone who asks receives; he who seeks finds; and to him who knocks, the door will be opened. . . how much more will your Father in heaven give good gifts to those who ask him!"* —MATTHEW 7:7-8, 11

1. How many times in Matthew 7:7-8 does Jesus encourage us, in different words, to pray? How many times does he promise that our prayers will be granted? Is there any significance in this repetition?

2. Is Jesus challenging us in the above verses to ask and seek and knock for ourselves, or for others? Support your answer from the words of the passage above.

3. What do you think ask-ers will receive? What will seekers find? Where will knockers gain entrance? How important to us are the things that we receive, find, or gain entrance to?

4. If you were a parent whose children didn't want the good gifts you offered them enough to ask for them, what would you do?

5. Why might the Father choose *not* to give his spiritual riches to believers who don't ask?

CLOSING PRAYER TIME   (10 MINUTES IN SMALL GROUPS)

Following are twelve very valuable spiritual blessings that are important to every Christian. God will *always* give these blessings to believers who sincerely ask for them: love, joy, peace, faith, hope, grace, mercy, wisdom, self-control, perseverance, spiritual empowerment, Spirit-filling.

Spend time asking for these blessings in prayer, one at a time, starting with the ones that you most need or most desire. Each time you ask for a particular blessing, thank God for it immediately, knowing for sure that he will give it.

PERSONAL PRAYER THIS WEEK

Regularly address God as "Father" at the beginning of your prayers this week. Pause for a few moments after you address God to revel in the wonder of this your Father/child relationship. Recall the Father's fondness for you and his complete devotion to your well-being. Then go on in your prayer.

SUGGESTED READING THIS WEEK

Read the five Week Four devotions in *The Joy of Prayer* (pp. 45-55)

※

WEEK FIVE

Prayer and Spiritual Warfare

In this session we will learn that
- ◆ true prayer will pit us against the evil one.
- ◆ prayer is a mighty force in defeating Satan.
- ◆ prayer is a form of spiritual protection.
- ◆ Jesus delegates spiritual authority to praying Christians.

DVD INTRODUCTION   (20 MINUTES)

The Son of God came to destroy the works of the devil

He went around doing good and healing all who were under the power of the devil. —ACTS 10:38

By his death he [destroyed] him who holds the power of death—that is, the devil—and [freed] those who all their lives were held in slavery by their fear of death." —HEBREWS 2:14-15

- ◆ Christ chooses to continue his saving work and to _____ Satan through our prayers.
- ◆ It is_____ , not our prayers, that actually defeats Satan.
  "I will do whatever you ask in my name." —JOHN 14:13

Prayer is a mighty force in defeating Satan

- ◆ We are at war with an enemy that is too _____ for us.
- ◆ True prayer will _____ _____ against the forces of evil in the world.
- ◆ Through prayer we can gain _____ over evil.

Prayer is a form of spiritual protection

- ◆ Jesus taught us to pray "_____ us from the evil one."
- ◆ Jesus prayed for the _____ of his disciples.
  "Holy Father, protect them by the power of your name—the name you gave

*me—so that they may be one as we are one. . . . My prayer is not that you
take them out of the world but that you protect them from the evil one."*

—JOHN 17:11, 15

◆ Prayer is a way for believers to "_____ _____"
against the forces of evil in the world and to protect each other.

*. . . be strong in the Lord and in his mighty power. . . . take your stand
against the devil's schemes. . . . Stand firm then . . . with this in mind, be
alert and always keep on praying for all the saints.*

—EPHESIANS 6:10-11, 14, 18

Jesus delegates spiritual authority to praying Christians

◆ Spiritual authority is the right to give _____ and
enforce _____ in the spiritual realm.

*Jesus . . . gave them power and authority to drive out all demons and to cure
diseases, and he sent them out to preach. . . .* —LUKE 9:1-2

*The seventy-two returned with joy and said, "Lord even the demons submit
to us in your name." He replied, "I saw Satan fall like lightning from heaven.
I have given you authority to trample on snakes and scorpions and to overcome all the power of the enemy. . . ."* —LUKE 10:17-19

◆ Jesus _____ spiritual authority to his followers.

◆ Handled correctly spiritual authority is a powerful_____.

*[Jesus'] disciples asked him privately, "Why couldn't we drive [the demon]
out?" He replied, "This kind can come out only by prayer."*

—MARK 9:28-29

GROUP INTERACTION   (10-15 MINUTES)

React

Do most Christians you know operate with a "peacetime casualness" or with
an awareness that we are at war with a ruthless, invisible enemy? What is the
evidence? How could we increase our awareness of the enemy?

Share

Where do you see the devil working in the world today? How might he be
working in your church? In your family? What is he trying to do in your life?

Discuss

Is it better to be very conscious of the devil's activities in the world today or little conscious of him? What's the danger of being very conscious of him? Of being little conscious of him?

BIBLE STUDY   (10-15 MINUTES)

The reason the Son of God appeared was to destroy the devil's work.
—1 JOHN 3:8

Jesus of Nazareth. . . went around doing good and healing all who were under the power of the devil, because God was with him. —ACTS 10:38

(Christ) having disarmed the powers and authorities. . . made a public spectacle of them, triumphing over them by the cross. —COLOSSIANS 2:13, 15

"And lead us not into temptation, but deliver us from the evil one."
—MATTHEW 6:13

"Anyone who has faith in me will do what I have been doing. . . because I am going to the Father. And I will do whatever you ask in my name."
—JOHN 14:12-13

---

1. According to the verses above, Jesus came to earth to deal with what major problem?

2. What kinds of things did Jesus *do* to triumph over Satan and his evil forces? Are there things that we can *do* in order to triumph over Satan?

3. According to John 14:12-14, how can we do works like those Jesus did on earth? Does that include works that defeat the devil?

4. How is Jesus, now enthroned, involved in the ongoing work of defeating the devil? When the devil is defeated because we pray to Christ, are *we* doing the defeating? Is *Jesus*? Or is it both?

5. Why should we expect Jesus to eagerly hear and answer our "spiritual warfare" prayers?

Closing Prayer Time   (10 minutes in small groups)

Reflect

Try to name at least five specific ways the evil one works in the world today.

- _____
- _____
- _____
- _____
- _____

In your small group **pray** for Christ and his church to triumph over each of the devil's evil schemes that you have named. Let the Holy Spirit lead you to pray about additional efforts of Satan that need to be thwarted.

Personal Prayer This Week

Pray this week for Christ to triumph in all of the areas that you have listed above. Add to your list additional areas that the Spirit brings to mind. Pray especially for the *persons* who are being harmed physically or spiritually by the devil's schemes and his "spiritual forces of evil." Pray that all of God's people will be able to stand and to "be strong in the Lord and the strength of his might" (Ephesians 6:10, 18).

Suggested Reading This Week

Read the five *Week Five* devotions in *The Joy of Prayer* (pp. 57-67)

☼

WEEK SIX

Prayer and Fasting

In this session we will learn that
- ◆ fasting is a type of prayer that increases intimacy with the Father.
- ◆ fasting opens our hearts to the Spirit's guidance.
- ◆ fasting and prayer are key elements in divine protection and spiritual restoration.
- ◆ true fasting leads to joy.

DVD INTRODUCTION   (17 MINUTES)

Fasting is a type of prayer that increases intimacy with the Father

- ◆ Fasting is an _____ form of prayer.
- ◆ Fasting _____ the ties that bind us to the material world.
- ◆ Fasting gets us _____ to the heart of God.

  *"When you fast, do not look somber as the hypocrites do. . . they have received their reward in full. But when you fast, put oil on your head and wash your face, so that it will not be obvious to others that you are fasting, but only to your Father. . . and your Father, who sees what is done in secret, will reward you." —*MATTHEW 6:16-18 (TNIV)

Fasting opens our hearts to the Spirit's guidance

- ◆ Fasting _____ our spiritual hearing.

  *While they were worshiping the Lord and fasting, the Holy Spirit said, "Set apart for me Barnabas and Saul for the work to which I have called them." So after they had fasted and prayed, they placed their hands on them and sent them off. —*ACTS 13:2-3

  *Paul and Barnabas appointed elders for them in each church and, with prayer and fasting, committed them to the Lord. —*ACTS 14:23

◆ Fasting _____ _____ intrusive noises.

Fasting and prayer are key elements in divine protection and spiritual restoration

◆ God wants to _____ his people but we shouldn't expect him to do so without our asking.

◆ God _____ sin-fallen people who are truly repentant.

"Even now," declares the LORD, "return to me with all your heart, with fasting and weeping and mourning. Rend your heart and not your garments. Return to the LORD your God, for he is gracious and compassionate, slow to anger and abounding in love, and he relents from sending calamity."

—JOEL 2:12-13

True fasting leads to joy

◆ Sin is a_____ - _____.

◆ God is a_____ - _____. He blesses those whose hearts are broken over sin.

This is what the Lord Almighty says: "The fasts of the fourth, fifth, seventh and tenth months will become joyful and glad occasions and happy festivals for Judah. Therefore love truth and peace." —ZECHARIAH 8:19

GROUP INTERACTION   (10-15 MINUTES)

React

What are the most important things you learned about fasting from the introductory presentation?

Share

Share with each other about a time in your life when you experienced increased intimacy with the Father. Did prayer have anything to do with it?

Discuss

Agree or disagree: When God doesn't seem to be "hearing" our prayers, we should fast in order to convince him we are really serious and to get him to respond. Defend your answer.

BIBLE STUDY   (10-15 MINUTES)

"When you fast, do not look somber as the hypocrites do, for they disfigure their faces to show others they are fasting. Truly I tell you, they have received their reward in full. But when you fast, put oil on your head and wash your face, so that it will not be obvious to others that you are fasting, but only to your Father, who is unseen, and your Father, who sees what is done in secret, will reward you."

—MATTHEW 6:16-18 (TNIV)

1. According to Jesus, what is the wrong way to fast? What is wrong about it? What is the reward for wrong-way fasting?

2. What is the right way to fast? What's right about it? What is the nature of the reward Jesus promises?

3. What do we learn about fasting from these words of Jesus that would make us believe that it is a type of prayer? What do you suppose happens in our relationship with God if our fasting is "to the Father"?

4. Is it wrong to let others know that we are fasting? Why or why not?

CLOSING PRAYER TIME   (10 MINUTES IN SMALL GROUPS)

Share

Make a list of things you could give up in order to have more time and energy for God. Think of things like reading the newspaper, watching a TV program, listening to a radio broadcast, foregoing a snack or a meal, and so on. These are, in a way, types of fasting. Once you have a list, share briefly what you could put into these times that would draw you closer to the heart of God.

Pray

In a silent prayer time ask God to guide you in the matter of fasting. Let the Spirit prompt you to give up something, even temporarily, which would enhance your relationship with the Father. Commit to do anything he confirms in your heart and mind.

Report

Talk to group members about anything you think the Spirit is prompting you to do.

PERSONAL PRAYER THIS WEEK

Intentionally give up something each day in the coming week, whether large or small, in order to have more time and energy for God. Put activities into these gaps that will draw you closer to the heart of God. Take note of any "reward" God has for you.

SUGGESTED READING THIS WEEK

Read the five *Week Six* devotions in *The Joy of Prayer* (pp.69-79)

✺

WEEK SEVEN

Praying With Old Testament Saints

In this session we will learn that
- ◆ our prayers influence God.
- ◆ intercessors need to report for duty.
- ◆ a good prayer is one that will help us serve God better.
- ◆ parents are called to be priests for their family members.

DVD INTRODUCTION   (19 MINUTES)

Our prayers influence God

- ◆ Abraham, in his prayer for Sodom and Gomorrah, was able to
  _____God down from fifty to ten.

  Then the LORD said, "Shall I hide from Abraham what I am about to do?"
  —GENESIS 18:17

- ◆ Moses' prayer to spare Israel _____ God's mind.

  *"I have seen these people," the LORD said to Moses, "and they are a stiff-necked people. Now leave me alone so that my anger may burn against them and that I may destroy them." —*EXODUS 32:9-10

  *Then the LORD relented and did not bring on his people the disaster he had threatened. —*EXODUS 32:14

- ◆ Intercession does not overcome God's_____; it takes
  hold of his _____.

Intercessors ask God to intervene and then report for duty

- ◆ Nehemiah's prayer led to a challenging _____.

  For some days I mourned and fasted and prayed before the God of heaven.
  —NEHEMIAH 1:4

- ◆ Asking God to intervene does not eliminate human_____.

130

A good prayer is one that will help us serve God better

The LORD appeared to Solomon during the night in a dream, and God said, "Ask for whatever you want me to give you." —1 KINGS 3:5

◆ Solomon asked for _____ in order to be the best king he could be.

You have made your servant king. . . But I am only a little child and do not know how to carry out my duties. . . So give your servant a discerning heart to govern your people and to distinguish between right and wrong.

—1 KINGS 3:7, 9

◆ God is pleased when we ask for what we need to _____ him well.

◆ God sometimes chooses to be _____ beyond our asking.

The Lord was pleased that Solomon had asked for this. So God said to him. "Since you have asked for this and not for long life or wealth for yourself . . . I will do what you have asked. . . Moreover, I will give you what you have not asked for—both riches and honor." —1 KINGS 3:10-13

Parents are called to be priests for their family members

Early in the morning he (Job) would sacrifice a burnt offering for each of them (his sons & daughters), thinking, "Perhaps my children have sinned and cursed God in their hearts." This was Job's regular custom. —JOB 1:5

◆ Job prayed for the spiritual well-being of his _____ and _____.

◆ Job prayed for them in their_____.

◆ Job prayed for them with _____ and _____.

GROUP INTERACTION   (10-15 MINUTES)

React

What important things do we learn about *God* from the way he responds to prayer? What do we learn about prayer?

Share

Which of the following Old Testament saints do you identify with most closely? Abraham, who prevailed with God; Moses, who changed God's mind; Nehemiah, who prayed and reported for duty; Solomon, who prayed for wisdom; Job, who prayed for his children. Why? Share your thoughts with your small group.

Discuss

How might history have been different if Nehemiah had not reported for duty? If Solomon had asked for wealth and long life instead of wisdom?

BIBLE STUDY   (10-15 MINUTES)

"As the LORD, the God of Israel, lives, whom I serve, there will be neither dew nor rain in the next few years except at my word." —1 KINGS 17:1

Elijah said to Ahab, ". . . there is the sound of a heavy rain." So Ahab went off to eat and drink, but Elijah climbed to the top of Carmel, bent down to the ground and put his face between his knees.

"Go and look toward the sea," he told his servant. And he went up and looked.

"There is nothing there," he said.

Seven times Elijah said, "Go back."

The seventh time the servant reported, "A cloud as small as a man's hand is rising from the sea." . . . the sky grew black with clouds, the wind rose, a heavy rain came on. . . . —1 KINGS 18:41-45

The prayer of a righteous person is powerful and effective. Elijah was a man just like us. He prayed earnestly that it would not rain, and it did not rain on the land for three and a half years. Again he prayed, and the heavens gave rain, and the earth produced its crops. —JAMES 5:16-18

---

1. Based on this episode, what did Elijah believe about prayer?

2. Why do you think God waited to send rain until Elijah had prayed *seven* times?

3. Why do you suppose Elijah sent his servant back to check the sky each time after he had prayed?

4. What is the main lesson to be learned from Elijah's intercession? Could Ahab have secured the same results as Elijah if he had prayed?

5. When it comes to intercessory prayer power, how do you compare with Elijah?

CLOSING PRAYER TIME   (10 MINUTES IN SMALL GROUPS)

What things could, and perhaps should, be changed in your church by means of powerful intercessory prayer. Think about issues related to unity, outreach, stewardship, worship, devotion to prayer, leadership, and so on.

Pray together about some of the issues that you have identified. Does God want you to continue to pray about these things?

PERSONAL PRAYER THIS WEEK

Remember as you pray this week that your intercessory prayers are "powerful and effective." (Note the Greek word for powerful can also be translated as strong, prevailing, or availing much.) Persist in prayer as Elijah did. Watch for the "small cloud" answers. *Prepare for rain.*

SUGGESTED READING THIS WEEK

Read the five *Week Seven* devotions in *The Joy of Prayer* (pp. 81-91)

※

WEEK EIGHT

The Praying Church

In this session we will learn that
- ◆ the New Testament Church was devoted to prayer.
- ◆ corporate prayer is highly valued.
- ◆ good prayer meetings are God-focused.

DVD INTRODUCTION (17 MINUTES)

The New Testament Church was devoted to prayer

◆ The early Christians demonstrated _____ to prayer.

*These all . . . were continually **devoting** themselves to prayer.*
—ACTS 1:14 (NASB)

*They **devoted** themselves. . . to prayer.* —ACTS 2:42

*They (leaders) **devoted** themselves. . . to prayer.* —ACTS 6:4 (NASB)

***Devote** yourselves to prayer.* —COLOSSIANS 4:2

*Be **devoted to** prayer.* —ROMANS 12:12 (NASB)

*With this in mind, be alert, and pray **devotedly** for all the saints.*
—EPHESIANS 6:18

◆ Early Christians found their _____ _____ in the life and teachings of Jesus.

Very early in the morning, while it was still dark, Jesus got up. . . and went off to a solitary place, where he prayed. —MARK 1:35

But Jesus often withdrew to lonely places and prayed. —LUKE 5:16

Corporate prayer is highly valued

◆ Corporate prayer was a _____ _____ for the early church.

134

◆ Their corporate prayer was "_____" prayer.

"I tell you that if two of you on earth agree about anything you ask for, it will be done for you by my Father in heaven." —MATTHEW 18:19

◆ Jesus is _____ when we come together in prayer.

"For where two or three come together in my name, there am I with them."
—MATTHEW 18:20

◆ Christ promises to _____ when we pray "agreeing" prayers.

Good prayer meetings are God-focused

◆ God-focused prayers are full of_____.

They raised their voices together in prayer to God. "Sovereign Lord," they said, "you made the heaven and the earth and the sea, and everything in them. You spoke by the Holy Spirit through the mouth of your servant, our father David." —ACTS 4:24-25

◆ God-focused prayer strengthens_____.
◆ God-focused prayer gives_____.

GROUP INTERACTION   (10-15 MINUTES)

React

How do the prayer practices of your church compare to those of the first church of Jerusalem? How are they alike? How do they differ?

Share

When a church leader at the front of an auditorium leads in prayer, what goes on in your head? Is your mind wandering? Are you just listening? Are you really praying with the leader? Try to put percentages on these options. Share with each other.

Discuss

It is widely believed that church prayer meetings are unnecessary since "we can pray just as well at home." What do you think of that idea? Is anything gained in corporate prayer?

BIBLE STUDY   (10-15 MINUTES)

Then they called them in again and commanded them not to speak or teach at all in the name of Jesus. . . On their release, Peter and John went back to their own people and reported all that the chief priests and elders had said to them. When they heard this, they raised their voices together in prayer to God. "Sovereign Lord," they said, "you made the heaven and the earth and the sea, and everything in them. You spoke by the Holy Spirit through the mouth of your servant, our father David:

"Why do the nations rage
and the peoples plot in vain?
The kings of the earth take their stand
and the rulers gather together against the Lord
and against his Anointed One'

Now, Lord consider their threats and enable your servants to speak your word with great boldness. . . After they prayed, the place where they were meeting was shaken. And they were all filled with the Holy Spirit and spoke the word of God boldly. . . With great power the apostles continued to testify to the resurrection of the Lord Jesus, and much grace was upon them all.

—ACTS 4:18, 23-26, 29, 31, 33

---

1. Identify several noteworthy features about this prayer meeting. Which of these could be transferable to today? Which might not be transferable?

2. What did they find in David's psalm that was important to them at this very time? What was the bedrock of their faith?

3. What kind of message did the shaking of their meeting place communicate to them? Do you think it made them fearful or confident?

4. What seems to have been their greatest concern?

5. What connection is there between their request in verse 29 and what is reported in verses 31 and 33?

CLOSING PRAYER TIME (10 MINUTES IN SMALL GROUPS)

Give each person in the group opportunity to share
- a prayer joy (something that is working).
- a prayer weakness (an area of struggle or failure).
- a prayer goal (something you aspire to).

In prayer rejoice with the joys of others in your group. Cover each other in your areas of struggle. Support each other in your goals.

PERSONAL PRAYER THIS WEEK

Throughout the next week, thank God for the gains you enjoy. Confess your weak areas and work through any failure. Commit to the goals you've set for yourself. And in all of this, pray for the help of the Holy Spirit.

SUGGESTED READING THIS WEEK

Read the five *Week Eight* devotions in *The Joy of Prayer* (pp. 93-103).

꙳

LEADER NOTES

Leader Preparation Each Week

Prepare for the lesson by viewing in advance the DVD and working through the "Group Interaction" and "Bible Study" segments on your own. Make sure you understand and are comfortable with the "Closing Prayer Time" suggestions. Be prepared to underscore the importance of the "Personal Prayer This Week" and to encourage the "Suggested Reading" assignment. Work ahead of the group and complete the "Suggested Reading" assignment (five devotionals) before the group session—even though the rest of the group will read these devotionals the week following the session. Familiarity with the content of the five devotionals will give you a head start and help you lead the group. Prepare this way for each lesson.

Before you watch the DVD during each session
- invite feedback on the "Personal Prayer" assignment and the five devotionals from the past week (this will not apply the first week).
- read aloud the section "In this session we will learn that . . ." before viewing the DVD.
- introduce the "React" questions in the "Group Interaction" section before viewing the DVD.
- make sure group members have found the outline for the "DVD Introduction" in the study guide portion of the book and have a pencil or pen ready to take notes.

During each session the leader should
- read the questions for discussion and invite responses.
- invite someone to read the passage for the Bible study.
- pace the discussion so that each segment gets enough time.
- involve as many group members as possible in discussion and prayer.
- suggest dividing into small groups for closing prayer times if the group is large.
- underscore the value of the "Personal Prayer Time" suggestions for each week.

◆ remind group members of the "Suggested Reading This Week" assignments.

Week One: Leader

◆ Begin the session with a prayer reflecting the theme of the lesson you're about to study.

◆ Take some time for group members to get acquainted with each other. Consider using an icebreaker.

WATCH THE "DVD INTRODUCTION."

GROUP INTERACTION   (10-15 MINUTES)

The three "Group Interaction" questions have different purposes.

◆ **React**: This question gives the group a chance to express thoughts or reactions that relate to the presentation. Read the question aloud and give the group time to answer. Keep the whole group together (if it is not too large) for this question.

◆ **Share**: This question encourages group members to talk about themselves in some way that relates to the session theme. Divide into small groups of 4-5 persons for this share time. Allow 5-6 minutes before transitioning them to the "Discuss Question."

◆ **Discuss**: This question is intended to be thought-provoking and open-ended. There may not be a right or wrong answer. This question is also best done in a small group of 4-5 persons. End discussion time after 5 or 6 minutes. Invite comments or questions from the small groups that might be of interest to the whole group.

BIBLE STUDY

In the Bible study time you will do an inductive study of a Bible passage related directly to the lesson theme. The best way for you to prepare is to try to answer each question for yourself in advance. Start this section with your group by reading the passage aloud or having a group member read it. Proceed through the questions by reading each question aloud before you try to answer it. Let the questions direct the study. Give the group time to interact before giving your own answer. In some cases you may want to summarize the shared ideas into a single coherent thought before moving on to the next question. Watch the time. Keep things moving!

◆ **About the Questions**: Keeping the discussion on track will be easier if you read the five Week One devotionals in advance. For additional help see *Day 3* and *Day 4* of Week Four: *Praying Jesus Way*.

CLOSING PRAYER TIME

Encourage people to pray one- or two-sentence prayers during this prayer time. Suggest that they may contribute more than once. If the group is large, divide into smaller groups. Groups comprised of 6 or 7 persons will allow those who feel uncomfortable praying aloud in a small group, the option of praying silently.

PERSONAL PRAYER THIS WEEK

Underscore the value of a personal prayer time and the suggestions given. Promise to give group members time during your next session to report their experiences.

SUGGESTED READING

Encourage everyone to read the five devotionals, Week One: *The Joy of Prayer,* and to take enough time to work through the "Think," "Pray," and "Act" sections each day.

Week Two: Leader

◆ Begin by inviting feedback on their "Personal Prayer" assignment for the past week and on the five Week One devotionals they have read.

◆ Offer an opening prayer that reflects the lesson you are about to study.

DVD INTRODUCTION

◆ Read the "React" question before the group watches the DVD, so they can be processing the question during the DVD.

◆ Make sure they have opened their study guides to the "DVD Introduction" outline.

GROUP INTERACTION

◆ **About the Discuss Question**: When we pray to "God," we are really communicating with all three Persons of the Godhead.

BIBLE STUDY

◆ **About the Questions**: Make sure you have looked at *Day 4*: "Praying for the Spirit" before you lead the group through these questions.

PERSONAL PRAYER THIS WEEK

Underscore the value of the personal prayer time and the suggestions given. Promise once again to give group members time at the beginning of the next session to report their experiences of the past week.

SUGGESTED READING

Build anticipation for Week Two: *Praying With the Trinity* by reporting on your own experience using these devotions.

Week Three: Leader

◆ Remember to give group members an opportunity, as you begin this session, to report on their personal prayer experiences of the past week or on their experience in using the devotionals.

◆ In your opening prayer give glory to the Father, the Son, and the Holy Spirit for the ways in which they are engaged in prayer and ask for their help.

GROUP INTERACTION

◆ **About the Share Question**: A surprising number of people have "heard" the Spirit speak to them in personal ways but have never shared the experience with anyone, because they fear what the other person(s) would think. This is a great opportunity for them to share some of their "hearing" stories.

BIBLE STUDY

◆ **About the Questions**: Make sure you have looked at *Day 1*: "Does God Still Speak Today" and *Day 4*: "Is That Really You God?" before you lead the group through these questions.

CLOSING PRAYER TIME

If the group is large, divide into small groups.

PERSONAL PRAYER THIS WEEK

Emphasize the value of this take-home assignment. Suggest a "report back" time at the beginning of your next session.

SUGGESTED READING

Stir everyone's interest in the devotional readings for Week Three: *Hearing God in Prayer* by sharing one important insight these devotions gave you.

Week Four: Leader

◆ Give group members an opportunity at the beginning to report on their "listening" experience of the past week.

GROUP INTERACTION

◆ **About the Share Question**: Make sure the group spends some serious time on the second of these two questions and doesn't get stuck on the first question.

BIBLE STUDY

◆ **About the Questions**: Make sure you have looked at *Day 3*: "The Master Key of Prayer" before leading the group through these questions.

CLOSING PRAYER TIME

This "Closing Prayer Time" can be done individually or in small groups.

PERSONAL PRAYER THIS WEEK

Present a couple of thoughts you garnered from reading *Day 1*: "Praying Like a Child" as you encourage them to try this prayer suggestion.

Week Five: Leader

◆ Give group members time to report on their prayer experience and their devotional reading in the past week.

◆ Demonstrate your familiarity with the Father/child prayer relationship in the way you lead the opening prayer.

DVD INTRODUCTION

Before starting the DVD ask the group why they think Jesus Christ came into the world.

GROUP INTERACTION

◆ **About the Share Question**: The idea of "peacetime casualness" is referenced in *Day 2*: "Prayer and Spiritual Struggle."

◆ **About the Discuss Question**: Review *Day 3*: "Prayer and Spiritual Protection" before you lead the group in this discussion.

BIBLE STUDY

◆ **About the Questions**: Having a good grasp of the teachings in Week Five's devotions will help you lead the group through this study.

CLOSING PRAYER TIME

Divide into small groups if most members are comfortable verbalizing prayer.

This prayer can also be done in a large group. To relieve some people's uneasiness about when and how they might contribute, ask for volunteers to pray about certain issues before the prayer time begins.

PERSONAL PRAYER THIS WEEK

Read *Day 2*: "Prayer and Spiritual Struggle" in advance and challenge the group members with the words of Ephesians 6:18 (*always keep on praying for all the saints*) to pray for each other, as well as for themselves in the coming week.

SUGGESTED READING THIS WEEK

Share any fresh insights you have from reading in advance the five devotionals on "Prayer and Spiritual Warfare." This encourages group members to persist in their devotional reading.

Week Six: Leader

◆ Ask group members if they have a greater awareness of the forces of evil as a result of the past week's personal prayer exercise. Did the Spirit bring to mind additional areas to pray about?

◆ In your opening prayer give thanks for Christ's defeat of the powers of darkness.

DVD INTRODUCTION

Make one or two preview comments about the DVD as you begin.

BIBLE STUDY

◆ **About the Questions**: Read *Day 1*: "Prayer, Fasting, and God's Heart" before leading this Bible study time.

CLOSING PRAYER

This "Closing Prayer Time" is different from what you have done before in this group. Familiarize yourself before introducing it.

PERSONAL PRAYER THIS WEEK

Underscore the value of the "Personal Prayer" challenge. Report your experience to the group if you have done this in advance.

Week Seven: Leader

◆ Inquire about group members' fasting experiences last week.
◆ Reflect in your opening prayer some of the learnings gained during the previous six weeks.

DVD INTRODUCTION

Invite group members to look at the "Share" question before you start the DVD, so they can think about how to answer that question for themselves.

CLOSING PRAYER TIME

Invite members to share personal prayer concerns. Pray for these concerns.

Week Eight: Leader

GROUP INTERACTION

◆ **About the Discussion Question**: In answering this question, consider the values of a corporate prayer meeting when believers are led in prayer through the prayers of others, gain a wider awareness of persons and concerns to be prayed for, pray out of their different spiritual gifts and passions, and support each other in prayer.

BIBLE STUDY

◆ **Questions:** If response is slow, ask group members to read the verses aloud.

SUGGESTED READING THIS WEEK

This week you and your group will complete the reading of *The Joy of Prayer*. Think about going through the book a second time. It takes time and repetition to lock in good devotional habits.